# Billionaire In Training

### Because Millionaire just isn't rich enough ...

## By

# BRADLEY J. SUGARS
## Edited by Grant McDuling

*ACTION* International *Pty Ltd*

ISBN 0-9580932-0-2
FIRST EDITION

Published by *ACTION International* Pty Ltd
GPO Box 1340 Brisbane, QLD 4001
Phone: +61 (0) 7 3368 2525
Fax: +61 (0)  7 3368 2535
www.action-international.com

Design & Layout by *ACTION International* **Design** Pty Ltd
Phone: +61 (0) 7 3367 3222  Website: www.ai-design.com.au

Distributed by *ACTION International* for further information
Phone: +61 (0) 7 3368 2525  Website: www.action-international.com

Printed in Australia by Fergies Image to Press

*To those who love business like I do ...*

*may it be as tough but kind to you as it has to me ...*

Years ago, when I was starting out in business and was still struggling to make ends meet, I thought becoming a millionaire was the ultimate financial goal. My perception changed, however, when I became a millionaire ... it was then I discovered being a millionaire just wasn't rich ...

With this book I am going to teach you how to become a millionaire ... then a deca-millionaire ... then a centa-millionaire and then the ultimate ... a BILLIONAIRE!

All the best ...

*Brad Sugars*

# ▌ Acknowledgments

When you choose to be an entrepreneur you choose an amazingly passionate and challenging life. It's through that passion that you learn so much, but it's through the challenges that you grow so much.

I'd like to first of all thank my writing team, Grant McDuling for his hours of dedicated translation of my ideas and notes into something of substance and context. To Sandra Fritz, for her passion for editing and the finer details. And, to Shaun Ford for his tiring pursuit of graphic perfection and meeting deadlines.

To my team at Action International all over the world, thanks for making a difference in the lives of others every day. Coaching is not the easiest work but that's why it's so rewarding. To my team of ML's and Coaches ... you are the people that make Action truly the World's #1 Business Coaching Team every day ...

To my other partners in all my other companies, Nic, Sonya and Trevor in Action Planning, Mark Thomas in Franchise Masters, Glen and Kerriane at Mr Rentals, Mike and Darlene at GlobePro's, Darren, Jackie and Peter at Mars Venus Coaching, Shaun Ford at Action International Design, my wife Jenny at MBT Skin Therapy, Phil and Dave at Entrepreneurs Success Centre ... You all make my life and work so much more enjoyable.

To my teachers' ... Mardi, you keep me on track and heart centred. Mark and Sharon, you allow me to be who I am and protect me from the world. Mum and Dad, you remind me of what's important and keep me as down to earth as one can be. To all the writers of all the books, the teaches of all the seminars and the mistake makers who lead the way, thank-you.

Finally to my beautiful wife Jenny and daughter Coby ... you both make me so happy to be alive that I wake with a smile when I hear your voices.

# ▌CONTENTS

# ▌Introduction

There are so many different ways to make it in business - so many different ways through which you can reap the rewards of entrepreneurial success. Yet very few people ever learn what it takes, and for some strange reason, fewer still will ever use what they've learnt.

Congratulations on taking the first step towards learning how you can succeed in the world of entrepreneurial business. The first step is to invest in the knowledge, the second is to absorb the knowledge, and the third and most important step, as you read and in particular when you finish reading, is to take ACTION.

In our dreams we are all winners, reality just narrows down the competition. The world of business is, by nature, a competitive one, but it is still just a game.

This book is like a play-book: a book designed to save you a lot of mistakes, a book designed to get you into the game at a much faster pace and at a much higher level. It is a street-wise book designed to give you the tools you need to make your dreams come true much sooner than you might have anticipated.

But to go forward, we first must look way back into the past - back into feudal times when the phrase 'survival of the fittest' was more than just a theory. It was for real.

Early on in feudal times when business was a little more basic than it is today and when people wished for the simple things like food, shelter and water, the fundamentals of our current business and economic system began to take shape.

This is a history that has more impact on the way people go about working and making money today than most would realize.

Of course, I'm not going to relate it as it's written in the history books. I want to teach it to you in a way that allows you to both understand why you're currently getting the financial results you're getting right now, and to take the leaps and bounds necessary to make sure your wildest financial dreams become a reality.

So, let's take a very careful, but simplistic, look at it.

In feudal times the leader of each clan was, to put it bluntly, the biggest and strongest person around. Why? Simply because the biggest, strongest is able to physically make their point heard to anyone who might consider challenging him or her. Things didn't change much in those days and any one leader could rule for a lifetime.

Business was also very simple then as the stability of the leader and the unchanging nature of the times meant everyone knew their place in life. Most people were content just to keep on producing over their very short life spans.

That was until the spear was invented.

Now, technology began to have an impact on the group. The most proficient spear user became the potential new leader. Then the bow and arrow came along, followed by body armour. This development necessitated the invention of an even more sophisticated weapon – the gun.

The most effective user of this new technology (the bow and arrow, the gun, etc) could now quite easily become the new leader.

As more and more inventions came to pass, and more and more products hit the market place, business and staying in charge began to tax the minds of the leaders.

Here's where it all gets interesting … the leaders realized one very important fact. If they were to stay on as leader, they needed to 'think hard' rather than to 'work hard'.

You see, if the leader was the smartest as well as the biggest person around, something truly extraordinary happened. The leader enrolled the inventors, those who knew things the leader didn't, as employees.

The leaders now made sure these spears were only made for them, the guns were only made for them. As a result, another amazing thing happened.

The leader taught each employee to be a Master Specialist. He then encouraged his Master Specialists to take on apprentices so they could teach other people to specialize in the same skills. By doing so, they started a trend where everyone aspired to learning a trade and getting a job rather than becoming a landowner.

Eventually we moved from an agrarian-based society to a manufacturing-based one. The leader still employed all the specialists who knew more than he did in certain areas. Schools were built to teach people from early on how to be good, how to do as they were told, how to fit into society and how to get a good job (as a Specialist).

Society started to teach us a good citizen was someone with a good education and a good job.

Eventually colleges and universities appeared, making us specialize even more. Over time we've been taught to specialize into the tiniest fields of expertise and thus become even better employees.

You see, in the agrarian age, you made the most money as a landowner, not as a specialist worker. In the manufacturing age, you made the most money if you owned the manufacturing plant, not as a specialist worker in the plant.

Those who specialized have always worked for those who led – in other words, those who generalized led those who specialized. However, the high cost of land ownership, and then plant ownership, stopped most from progressing from worker to owner.

Yet now, in the information age, you make the most money if you own, or simply have, the best information. And, information is not only available in abundance; it's relatively cheap.

In other words, breaking free from the specialist mould has never been easier.

Let me take this one step further …

With most people being taught to specialize, to follow orders, to conform, to fit in, and to get a good job with a good salary, we've created a monster when it comes to letting people start their own businesses.

You see we've been taught to do the opposite of thinking for ourselves, to do the opposite of getting rich, and in most cases to do the opposite of learning how to be a true entrepreneur.

A true entrepreneur is best described by this fable about Henry Ford. I'm sure the story has changed a little over the years but there's still a level of truth to it. As the story goes, a major newspaper defamed Mr. Ford when it published an article that portrayed him as 'ignorant'.

Mr. Ford took them to court and whilst on the stand, he was questioned at length by the newspaper's legal counsel. Question after question was put to him, and he only had answers to a few of them. Thus, concluded the attorney as he presented his case to the jury: "Mr. Ford is ignorant."

Ford's own lawyer then asked some questions.

"Mr. Ford, when you need to know the answer to any of the previous questions, what do you do?"

Ford's reply teaches us one of the secrets to true entrepreneurial success. This is a common sense secret that is the opposite of what we're taught as a specialist employee.

"When I need to know about finance, I call in my finance manager and ask him all the questions I need to have answered. The same goes for any other subject," Ford replied.

In other words, the smartest leaders in the world employ specialists who are smarter than they are.

Henry Ford knew what every great entrepreneur knows …

Being an entrepreneur is about becoming a generalist, rather than a specialist.

A specialist (often known as an employee) is easily replaceable. A specialist is taught to follow. A specialist ends up working for a living, rather than living a life.

Let me explain …

Working in a job, you have about 1/3rd of your pay taken off in taxes, about 1/3rd taken to pay for your mortgage or rent, even more to pay for your car/s and so on. Eventually you've got just enough left over to EXIST on.

Generalists, on the other hand, think for themselves. They are great leaders, they take on the risks and reap the rewards from things like tax deductions and more importantly, they collect long-term income from the work they do today. They also enjoy the profits, as well as so much more.

The generalist, the person I refer to as the entrepreneur, works today to make money for the long-term. They work to build wealth rather than make income.

In school, we're taught to learn exactly what we're told, how we were told it, and when we were told it. Plus, you'll get good grades as long as you repeat it back in your tests exactly as it was taught in the books.

Even teachers are taught to follow the system. In the military every soldier is taught to follow orders. Only the GENERAL(ist) is taught to think for him or herself and to make decisions.

In the business world, employees are taught to acquire higher and higher levels of education, to specialize, work hard, and make enough income to pay taxes, the mortgage, and then to exist until retirement.

True entrepreneurs, on the other hand, are required to be generalists, to think a lot and work a little, take profits, write expenses off before paying taxes, and live the life of their dreams …

In the truest sense of the word generalists are leaders. They live by the ideal that it's better to have 1% of one hundreds people's effort than 100% of their own.

Becoming a generalist is the first major task of anyone considering venturing into business for himself or herself.

It's the single biggest mindset change all employees who want to start their own business must make. Being the best at your trade, your profession or your job in no way means you'll succeed in the world of entrepreneurial business.

In fact, this is often the biggest hindrance to the success of most businesses. More on this later in the book.

# ▌My Story

For me the path to becoming a generalist entrepreneur was a little different than most.

My Dad decided I was going to be a businessman when he found me selling my Christmas presents to my brothers when I was only seven. The following year I'd become much smarter and worked out that if I just rented my toys to them for a day or two at a time, I got the money and the toys back afterwards.

I'm so glad now that I was a different kind of child, one who was so interested in business and money rather than just getting a job.

One other thing others may think of as a sin, but I now see as a virtue. I am UNEMPLOYABLE ... I found this out when I was 15 and tried to work a part-time job, not realizing that thinking for myself and outshining my boss wouldn't do me any favours.

It's been a long road since then, owning many different businesses of all shapes and sizes, being awarded an accounting degree, making a lot of money, losing a lot of money, investing a lot of money, travelling the globe several times over, teaching hundreds of thousands of business people, writing several best-selling books, building a world-wide conglomerate, and living a great life with amazing relationships with my family, friends and business colleagues.

I've owned companies involved in everything from business consulting, insurance and property investment at one end of the scale to dog food, ladies fashion retail, pizza manufacturing and wholesale at the other.

I was born, and have now truly become, the ultimate Generalist.

Every business I've owned, the 20 or so part and full-time jobs I had throughout my very short career as an employee, and everything else I've learned about life, love and wealth along the way, have all led me to believe one thing …

That the book you're about to read, and the information contained within it, is truly one of the fastest tracks to wealth creation you'll ever find.

You see, I've just turned 31 and it has provided me with all I ever dreamed it would, and more.

Unfortunately for the cynics, there's no good luck/bad luck story to go with it … it's just the plain fundamentals and some home truths about money and business I've picked up along the way. Nothing from a sage on a hill, or one particular mentor, but rather a lot of mentors, and a lot of people I've had the privilege to meet and learn from.

You see, everyone in the world knows more than you and I … about something. We just need to ask the right questions and listen long enough to find out what that 'something' is.

So, let me introduce you to my book.

In a moment I'm going to give you my fundamental truths on getting rich and why for most people (the Specialists), it's a long and arduous road, even when they do go into business for themselves.

People always ask me why no one ever taught this to them at school, and the answer is simple.

In the grand scheme of things, no one wants the majority of the population to know how to get rich - who would do the work and pay the taxes then? And, an even simpler reason, very few even know how to get rich, let alone how to teach it to others.

Next, I'll share with you my Five Levels of Entrepreneurs. I do this with one purpose in mind. To give you the ladder upon which you can climb to create your business and financial success. As you move from

Employee right through to Entrepreneur, you'll see not only the changes in skills required but also the changes in mindset you'll need to make.

You'll also get to see the differences in the way each and every level relates to money. No matter which of the Five Levels you're at right now, you'll almost immediately change the way you think when it comes to business, money and wealth. From here on you'll start to get the real-life understanding of the Generalist.

Then it's on to what I believe to be some of the most exciting business truths you'll ever get to learn. And, whether you're already in business or waiting in the wings, you'll soon be more excited than ever at the prospects of both financial success and, even more importantly, the freedom to do with your time what you will. This is where I teach you how to quickly jump to Level 4 – that of The Investor.

But firstly, I'll show you how to buy a business, with everything from where to get the cash and how to put together the deal, down to the fundamental rules you should never break when buying your own business, or businesses.

It's amazing how many people make the most fundamental mistake of buying a business in which they are good at the JOB in the business rather than choosing a business that has a good chance of making a high level of profit.

I want to teach you how to RUN a business, and then how to OWN a business, but not how to WORK in a business.

Next, we'll examine the most important areas you've just got to learn so you can build the business quickly and cost effectively. (Remember to play my board game 'Leverage: The Game of Business', or read my first book 'Instant Cashflow' for more on this.)

We'll go through the ways to boost income and profits, how to put together a team, how to set up systems, and most importantly, how to get the business to work without you even being there.

Third, you'll learn how to sell your business. I know you may not want to, but you've got to set it up so you can. This one lesson will be so powerful when you're ready to cash in and reap the rewards of having built up the sales and profits of the business.

Lastly we'll go through the four most important ideals any entrepreneur must learn in order to reap the true rewards business ownership has to offer. Just these four points will make sure you get started on the right foot on your road to entrepreneurial riches - on the right foot to becoming a Generalist.

One last point before we really get started …

It's easy to choose success over failure. It's easy to choose riches over poverty. In fact, it's easy to choose any dream over its dreary counterpart.

What's hard to do is to re-choose that same goal, that same dream, that same level of success every single day, every single hour, until it becomes a reality. You see while it's easy to choose success and riches, it's not easy to carry through with your thoughts every hour of every day.

It is simple (especially with what you're about to learn) to make your business and wealth dreams come true. You see if it were 'easy', as well as 'simple' then everyone would do it. Successful people choose to do what unsuccessful people don't do.

Choose to be one of the most successful people you know, and re-choose it every single hour of every single day for the rest of your life.

Enjoy.

# Part 1

# ▌ Getting Rich

Getting Rich is much simpler than most would realize. In fact, we really need to define the word 'rich' before we go on, so you can see what I see as we go through this book.

Most people's only relationship with money is of never having enough. Most people live a 'paycheck to paycheck' existence, and use this month's paycheck to pay off last month's bills.

A paycheck, no matter how big, cannot be defined as wealth or riches. So often people seem to mistake getting a bigger paycheck or salary for getting richer. Nothing could be further from the truth for more than 95% of the population. As you well know, most people spend every dollar they earn, and then some.

The first stage in your quest for riches is to get yourself to a stage where you've made enough investments over time to give you what I call a PASSIVE income rather than a paycheck existence. In other words, your investments and businesses make money whether you get out of bed or not.

At this stage I won't get into the details of where to invest - we'll be doing that shortly - but suffice to say this level of PASSIVE income is your first goal. To put this into perspective, this goal takes most people their entire working lives to achieve. The only time they have PASSIVE income is in their retirement at age 65+.

However, if you know what you're doing and you're diligent in your desire to create riches, this goal of having $2,000, $5,000 or even $10,000 a month in PASSIVE income can be achieved in about three years if you're quick, five if you're not, seven if you want to take it a little slower, and maybe a year or two longer if you're currently deeply in debt.

---

Waiting until you're 65 is crazy when, if you follow even just a few of the simple steps I'll show you, you can easily reach this goal in three to seven years or, as I did by the age of 25.

Now, I know most people I've met would be extremely happy with just this level of wealth. If you are, then that's great, but you're about to get a very rude shock when I show you how easy it is to move to the levels above this.

The next stage in your financial growth is what I call WEALTHY. In today's world a millionaire is merely wealthy, not rich. Becoming wealthy in the traditional way takes far too long. It's a very slow process that involves investing a modest percentage of your income over a long period of time. WEALTH comes when you not only have PASSIVE income, but also assets to back it up. Wealth comes when you've truly cemented your long-term PASSIVE income with the steadiness of PHYSICAL ASSET GROWTH.

Most people go about this the wrong way and try to build ASSETS before they build PASSIVE income. They think they should invest in real estate before they have developed passive income. They think they can jump steps and wonder why they stumble. The only vehicle you can use to get passive income is business, and you don't do it by running a business, but by selling businesses.

By understanding the Five Levels of Entrepreneurs, you'll quickly see why building assets before passive income slows your path to riches.

Wealth is all about physical assets. And the Number One physical asset you can have is PROPERTY. But let's first consider what I believe an asset to be. This may come as something of a shock to you.

Assets MUST have both CAPITAL GROWTH and INCOME. If they don't, then they are not assets.

Don't buy property first if you want to become wealthy, build passive income. Otherwise you're likely to become ASSET RICH and CASH POOR.

Beyond WEALTH lies RICH …

RICH usually comes through only one thing; paper assets. I want you to truly understand one simple fact; the RICHER you are, the less you pay for.

To be RICH, you need to have two things that will allow you to produce the third. You need a rather large CASHFLOW, (in a moment I'll share with you my strategies for this) and a solid PHYSICAL ASSET base (I will also show you how I achieve this in a moment.)

These two things combined allow you to create the third part of getting RICH … PAPER ASSETS.

What then are paper assets? They are things like shares, contracts, licenses, royalties and franchise documentation. Share floats are one of the best paper assets because you get to choose how many shares you get to keep.

And what is your cost for a paper asset? Generally ZERO. That's the beauty of it – it usually costs you nothing.

Let me give you an example. I recently sold *ACTION INTERNATIONAL'S* Master Franchise for London for a lot of money. Yet the cost to me was zero. But you need to understand if I hadn't taken things one step at a time and achieved Passive Income first, then Wealth, I wouldn't have been able to do this because I wouldn't have had the knowledge.

Now, I know that most people would be happy to be just WEALTHY … you know, lots of PASSIVE income and lots of ASSETS, but trust me when I say that the next step, the step to Level 5 of my Five Levels of Entrepreneurs is the truly rewarding one.

I'll get into a lot more details shortly, but for now, let's examine …

## Cashflow

Most people rely solely on their JOB for their cashflow. Notice I don't use the word income. You see income seems to imply some level of work or activity involved, and one of the central themes of everything you'll learn from me, is one of the keys to riches is actually having others do the work for you. By the way, JOB is just an acronym for 'Just Over Broke'.

Having a normal job, whether it's in your own business or someone else's, severely limits your CASHFLOW capabilities. Here's why …

It's only possible to work so many hours per day and make so many dollars per hour for your own personal labor. Thus a paycheck can only be for the number of hours you've worked multiplied by your hourly rate.

Yes, I know there are a handful of people on the planet who take home million dollar plus pay packets, but they've almost always already served 20 or so years at normal wage levels, and secondly, if they stopped working tomorrow, the paycheck stops.

Thus, we need to look for another method of bringing in massive amounts of CASHFLOW.

There is only one tool I recommend you use for creating CASHFLOW in your life… YOUR OWN BUSINESS.

It is by far and away the best tool for creating massive cashflow and having someone else do the work. Business is also, as you'll see later, one of the best ways to develop a large pool of capital with which you can invest in assets.

By the way, am I saying everyone should quit their job and buy his or her own business? To put it bluntly … YES.

Let me make one point very clear though …

Having a job definitely serves a purpose, in fact two purposes we'll go through in just a moment, but suffice to say you may not have to quit your job just yet …

So, why BUSINESS as our CASHFLOW generator?

Several reasons. Firstly and most importantly to me, it's FUN. I love to play the game. I love the challenge of marketing, team building, sales, accounting and cashflow management. I love doing deals. I love making decisions and I love being a leader. I also love the fact I get to deal with so many different things as well as so many of the same things. You'll fall in love with it too when you see the results it can get for you.

Secondly, where else can you get all of the tax benefits a business brings. Depending on your tax jurisdiction these will vary, but globally the tax system certainly favors those of us in business.

Thirdly, the revenue stream can jump massively in a couple of weeks, days and even hours. And, very often, a 10% increase in income will double or treble the profits, thus doubling or tripling the paper value of the company.

Fourthly, a little bit of knowledge goes a long way. It doesn't take much to out-perform your competitors in business. Like it or not, most business owners do a very poor job of running their businesses. So, I only need to do some basic common sense things to totally win in the minds of my customers.

Fifthly, you can get 30 days credit.

Sixthly, you can employ others.

Seventhly, once you've written the system, you've written the system.

The list goes on and on …

In case you hadn't guessed it, I love business. But most importantly, I love business because it meets my investment rules.

It grows in CAPITAL VALUE, and secondly, it throws off PASSIVE cashflow while still allowing me to draw a wage (if it makes economic and taxation sense.)

So, let's look at some other options for CASHFLOW generation that I do NOT want to focus on.

SHARE TRADING AND DAY TRADING …

This is a full-time job with little to no chance of building an asset you can sell later. Whilst it can be proven it is substantially skills-based rather than just 'taking a bet', you not only have to work almost full-time and have no business as an asset to sell later on, but you have two other drawbacks that remove me from wanting to do it.

Firstly, you have to use your own money. Yes, I know you can leverage some shares up to as much as 70% of their value these days, but the returns on leveraged shares are extremely average. And yes, I know you can option trade so there is a level of leverage, but does the fact it's a full-time job and you still have to invest at least a sizeable amount of your own cash mean it should be our primary focus? I think not.

Secondly, it doesn't meet my criteria to even qualify as an investment. That is, an investment must BOTH grow in capital value AND give off passive cashflow.

This brings me to the second option I do not want to concentrate on. It also happens to be one more and more people are choosing as their CASHFLOW generator.

PROPERTY …

Now, let me be clear … I LOVE PROPERTY … but NOT as a cashflow tool. A lot of people are training you to hunt high and low for CASHFLOW properties. Believe me they're out there in abundance, but rarely will it produce anywhere near the CASHFLOW a business can.

Property is great because the cashflow pays for the property, the tax deductions help you save on the money you make in business, and what's more, the bank helps you buy most of it.

However, to me property doesn't belong in the discussion about how to generate CASHFLOW – it belongs in the next part of our wealth discussion where we look at assets.

Remember, you can choose another tool for cashflow generation, but in my opinion, none will give you the returns in both capital growth and cashflow generation a business will, particularly once you have learned the strategies and ideas I teach.

So, let's take a closer look at …

## Assets

I make my money (cashflow) in business. And I keep my money (assets) growing in property. I love property for so many reasons, but let me be clear, the focus of this book is not property (for more on this, read my book Real Money, Real Estate), its focus is business. I'll keep that focus because one thing has become blatantly obvious to me when watching people going about wealth creation.

Buying property is easy. In fact, there are literally hundreds of companies waiting to show you what you should invest in (we'll cover that in just a moment) and thousands of great books on the subject. However, most people have a massive problem with their ability to invest in a property or two every month …

They don't have the CASHFLOW …

Their job only really allows them to buy another property every few years. To get RICH, and to get RICH fast, you need more CASHFLOW. More, so you can buy more ASSETS at a much faster pace.

The CASHFLOW gives you your deposit, it gives you your ability to get loans and what's more, it gives you the ability to stay cash rich as well as asset rich.

One of the biggest challenges faced by wage earners who are trying to get rich through property is the amount of time, measured in years, which it takes to get their first few properties. They buy their own home, then about seven years later their first investment property. It takes another four or five years to get the equity to a level where they can borrow for another. It then starts to speed up but by this time they're in their mid-forties. Thus, time hasn't had its effect by the time they're ready to retire, so many end up asset rich and cash poor.

Others may loose money on a house they'd bought. The story spreads, leading many to become scared and avoid investing in property altogether.

- That said, here are just a few of the many reasons I love property so much …

- You can buy it for much less than it's truly worth. For any one of a dozen reasons people will sell you a house for much less than it's worth at the time. They just can't, or don't want to, wait for a reasonable price.

- You can easily add value to a property with a few simple and cost effective renovation and clean-up techniques.

- You can get a tenant to pay for the majority of your purchase.

- A bank will lend you the majority of the money to buy it.

- You can get insurance for almost everything.

- The Government thanks you with substantial tax deductions for providing housing for the population.

- You can re-borrow against the value of the house at a later date to collect tax-free money.  Remember selling may incur tax, but re-borrowing never will.

- They're not making any more land.

- It just sits there and does very little except grow in value over the long term (I'll deal with comparisons to the stock market shortly).

And there's one other reason I absolutely love property.  It helps me to ...

## Get into Debt

That's right ... debt is good ... especially when it's paid for by someone else, and when it's buying me an appreciable asset.  Debt for STUFF is bad.  In fact, if you keep buying STUFF all you life, you can easily guess what you end up with ...

STUFF ALL.

A simple aside here:  Land appreciates in value and buildings depreciate in value.  Thus, invest in the dirt more than the building.  That's why I don't like units, unless I own the whole block.

So, why is debt good?

Put very simply, it's this:

If you invest $20,000 cash into a $100,000 property, you borrow $80,000 and we assume with the rental income and tax benefits, your mortgage (generally interest only for at least the first 3 to 5 years) and other expenses should balance out.

By the way, we haven't assumed you bought a house worth $120K for $100K by shopping around and negotiating well.

Let's assume the property only grows by 5% this year ... that's a $5,000 return on a $20,000 investment ... thus 25%. Now, it's hard to find a property that will ONLY return such small amounts (traditionally it's been about 10% globally), but I'm sure if you walk around with your eyes closed, you'll find some.

These are just a few of the reasons I love property. To read more about investing in property, read my book Real Money, Real Estate.

However, there are a few problems with what most people have been taught about money and property investing.

## Lies, Lies And More Lies

Let's start with an oldie but a goodie ...

Pay off your own home first. This has got to be one of the most insane pieces of advice I have ever come across. Let's take a look back in history to find out why ...

Back in 1929 when the stock market started to tumble several things all came together to cause a new paradigm around owning your own home outright.

I'll make this overly simplistic to illustrate the point.

The markets tumbled by approximately 30% in just one day. This wasn't such a bad thing in and of itself, but the majority of investors had borrowed about 90% of their investment funds ...

As a result, they now owed more than their stocks were worth. Their lenders made what is referred to as a Margin Call and asked for more cash to secure their investment. This in turn led to a run on the banks for cash.

You guessed it; the banks ran dry.

At the time the average house was priced around $4,000 or $5,000 and a common clause in mortgage documents gave the banks the right to demand full and final payment at any time. So, when the banks needed cash to give to borrowers who needed to pay for their shares, they called in the home loans.

But, as is the case today, most of us don't have the price of our house sitting around in cash. The writing was on the wall.

The banks started repossessing houses and putting people onto the street. The Brokers started to sell the stocks and shares to recoup their money, but there was one major problem.

No one had the money to buy either the repossessed houses or the shares no matter what the price. So, everything became relatively worthless, prices tumbled, people starved, yet one group survived with a roof over their heads - those who had paid off their own homes entirely.

So, from that generation on, 'Pay off your home first, then you'll be safe and secure,' became firmly entrenched as a piece of sound advice.

Great advice for the times, but times have changed. Let's look at some of the specifics.

In 1929 the government refused to print more money for fear of inflation. In 1987 when the same incidents started to occur, US Federal Reserve Chairman Greenspan declared that he would print enough cash so that the banks would not run dry. The panic stopped.

Mortgage documents have changed too, banks have tighter lending rules, and you can't borrow 90% to buy stocks and shares, accept in very specific circumstances.

The rules of the game have changed, so now it's time for our thinking to change as well.

While I'm on the trail of the so-called truth, let's talk about the hype of the Stock Market vs. Business vs. Property. By now you should be clearly aware of which two I support most.

Don't get me wrong; I've made great money through the stock market. GREAT MONEY …

But for my long-term plan … give me business for cashflow and property for assets.

Don't get sucked in by the sales hype put out by the brokerage firms telling you the stock market has outperformed property in percentage returns. All they're saying is your rental income isn't that great compared to the value of the whole house.

Back to our $100,000 example: Imagine you got $6,000 in rental income, you could say this means you got a 6% return on the $100,000 house. But, as we know, it was only $20,000 cash that you had to put in. So the very basic true return if you want a direct comparison is 6,000/20,000, which is 30%. There is no real way to compare the two without taking into account capital return, expenses, tax deductions and so on.

There are many ways to prove a financial point and we can all put a different spin on things, so just remember this: Brokers and brokerage firms get paid when you buy and sell shares and mutual funds, not when you invest in property, so of course they're going to suggest you buy shares.

Want my advice? I'm rich, I get no commission no matter what you buy, and I say invest in property … you work it out …

One last little lie I have to warn you about …

Far too many companies in today's market take a commission for selling you investment properties … whilst what they say is true, you will ultimately get a good deal. The best deals are out there waiting for those of us who've bothered to read one or two books on property, learn about what we are doing, and then put in the time to find the deals.

Don't be fooled, not all property deals are good deals. But given an ounce of training, and as one of my trainers taught me, enough leg work to physically see and learn from seeing at least 100 properties before you buy, will see you well on your way.

So, just to recap.

My recommendation is to get into business for CASHFLOW and then to use the money you make to INVEST in PROPERTY ...

Now let's get stuck into the 5 Levels of Entrepreneurs I promised so you can see how getting into business by my definition is most probably very different to the way you're thinking about it.

# Part 2

# ▌ The 5 Levels Of Entrepreneurs

So often I meet people who think they're in business for themselves, and yet by my definition, they're not. Let me explain ...

My definition of a business is the following:

A Commercial, Profitable, Enterprise that Works Without Me ...

Anything else has to be classified as something other than a true business.

As with most things in life, there are so many different levels to 'being in business'. Lots of people say they play sport, but at what level? Lots of people say they're in business, but once again, at what level?

It's not just 'getting into your own business' that will make you rich. Just as it's not just doing some exercises that will get you to the Olympics. There are specific strategies, skills and so many more things you'll need to follow to turn your business and wealth dreams into reality.

As you most probably know, it's quoted that 80% of businesses fail within five years of start up. I imagine these numbers are true, but I want you to remember this ...

Most businesses do not fail because the owner didn't work hard. They don't fail because the owner wants them to fail; they failed because the owner didn't know what to do. They failed because the owner never ever got past Level 2 on my Entrepreneurs scale and in most cases, because the owner remained ignorant of the rules of the game.

I've always believed business is a game ... and if you want to play the game, you'd better learn the rules. What's more, you'd better learn them from someone who's succeeded at the game. Not from the scorekeepers (accountants), the rule makers (lawyers), the spectators (employees), the money holders and collectors (bankers) and definitely not from other 'D' grade players (business owners who are just getting by or even failing).

You've got to learn the game from the best players and the best coaches.

It seems so simple when you look at it from this angle. This, of course, raises another question. Who are the best players? Who are the Level 5's in this Entrepreneurial game?

Before I answer that, I want to make one other point very clear.

Most people who fail in business can always find an excuse for their failure (some use fancy words like reasons), others just blame everyone around other than themselves, and others still just bury their head in some sort of denial of the predicament they are in.

These three ways; blame, excuse and denial, are very much a product of the employee 'specialist' mentality - they help you play the game of the employee where you just want to keep your job.

On the other hand, there is only one way you'll truly succeed in business. That is to throw out these ways, to stop playing the role of the VICTIM and to start to play the role of the VICTOR.

To learn, then do, make mistakes, take full responsibility for them, learn from them, correct, do some more, and so on - this is the path of a Generalist Entrepreneur.

Entrepreneurs truly take accountability and responsibility for their own lives and as one you'll realize for your life to change, YOU must change.

Thus, the reason for these 5 Levels of Entrepreneurs ...

They're designed to give you a framework that'll allow you to firstly understand yourself and the thoughts you have that got you to where you are now, but then most importantly, you'll get the tools to grow from where you are now to where you want to be.

Remember, it's usually not the major concept (getting into business) that helps you create massive success, it's the fine distinctions (these 5 Levels are a very big start), the small details you learn along the way that will allow you to jump from average to high performance.

So, let's get started ...

## Level Zero – The Employee

Almost everyone starts out here. It's neither good nor bad, even though you probably get the idea it's not my most recommended strategy for wealth creation.

You see, being an employee trains you to be almost the exact opposite of an entrepreneur. Let me explain ...

You go to school and learn to be good, do as you're told and get a good job. When you get the job, you're taught from Day One to follow directions, get better at your job and never question authority. Yet, as I think I've made quite clear, that's not the path of an entrepreneur.

Unfortunately for most people, the time they spend as an employee is wasted. It's generally spent in one of two ways:

Firstly, keeping your head down and not rocking the boat. These people seem to perceive if no one notices you, you can't get fired. This is very true in some government positions and major corporations. The other assumption that goes with this way of existing is an even more insane one in today's world, even though it may have been partially true in the past. The assumption is that time spent in a position brings about pay increases and promotions. Once again, still true in some organizations, but definitely not a path to wealth and riches.

Secondly, most people play the 'employee' game by continually working harder, longer hours and getting more and more specialized. They strive to learn more and more about their job, they get better and better at their work, and very often they move from one company to another or from one position to another. Sure, they may get pay rises all the time, but they usually continue to spend more than they earn throughout the entire period.

The one major assumption our friends in this position continue to make is a higher income equals more wealth.

Once again, nothing could be further from the truth. For most people in this position, a larger paycheck just gets them further and further into debt because of their increased borrowing capacity.

In other words, they also miss the entire point behind being an employee. So, let's take a look at what it is to be an employee from an Entrepreneurs point of view.


## The Entrepreneurial Mindset of a Level 0

There are so many fundamental thought patterns that show up in a group of employees. Some are extremely rare and others are a part of almost every employee you meet.

I'm just going to examine their five biggest beliefs that relate directly to money, wealth, and becoming an entrepreneur. Remember, every thought pattern or belief in some way assists you and in others limits you. Something that may make you a great employee will truly limit you as an entrepreneur.

Friends invited me over for dinner recently. They had also invited some other friends of theirs. Several of them turned out to be serious employees.

They would ask questions like: "Who do you work for?" "How much do you earn?" But the one I liked most of all was: "What car do you drive?"

Now, I don't mean to be rude, but to some I will be. These people fell into the category I call 'LOOKING GOOD, GOING NOWHERE ...'

They would rather look rich than be rich. Another way to describe their life would be to say that they live it second hand. They do everything to build an impression of themselves to the outside world, and when the outside world says it's true, they believe it - even though it's just an illusion they've created. A second-hand opinion.

So, often just changing a couple of simple thoughts or beliefs could dramatically affect not only their financial lives, but also their emotional lives.

With this in mind, let's find the essential beliefs that have them and other 'Level 0 Employees' trapped in that little mouse's wheel - always running; yet standing still.

Firstly, my biggest bug bear that's literally a guarantee of the eternal poor use of money. The belief is that 'STUFF' is more important than WEALTH.

And, you know the 'STUFF' I'm alluding to. It's that dress you bought last week that you really didn't need. Those new Nike running shoes you bought because you liked the colours. The STUFF you want, the STUFF that chews up all your money, the STUFF that seems SO important when you're buying it ... the STUFF that rarely matters when you realize you're broke.

I'll be as blunt as I can ... spend your entire life buying STUFF and you'll end up with STUFF ALL ...

Remember this ... People should be first on your priority scale, money and wealth second, and STUFF, or things, a very distant third.

Now, don't get me wrong, I own LOTS of STUFF ... but it's in proportion ... I also have lots of investments, cash, businesses, properties and so on ... WEALTH pays for my stuff whether I get out of bed or not.

By the way, whenever you want to buy STUFF ... you should learn how to make it a tax deduction.

Keep your 'STUFF' in perspective. Sure, have it, but don't become obsessed with it.

Onto the second 'Level 0' belief we need to look at: Your 'income' is representative of your wealth.

I think I've already beaten this one with a stick, but just in case I haven't made my case absolutely clear, let me go over it again.

Your income and your wealth are two entirely separate, and in most cases, non-related items. I've met people who make over a million dollars a year in salary yet they are still poor because they spend more than that million on STUFF.

And I've met a 22 year old young man who's never made more than $18,000 a year before tax and who has a net worth in excess of half a million dollars in his property portfolio.

Your income doesn't determine your wealth. It's what you do with your income that determines your wealth.

Remember, income does not equal wealth.

The third belief I want to examine and discard is this: Because I'm more intelligent, more skilled or more experienced, I have a higher chance of becoming wealthy.

Once again, I've met a lot of very poor professors and very rich high school drop-outs.

For some reason we've come to equate good grades, good training, or good skills as the key ingredient to success. This is especially so in the world of the 'Level 0 Employee'.

An entrepreneur knows that courage, taking action and leadership, are more important than scholastic intelligence.

In my world, my team of business coaches and I are continually working with people who 'thought they knew everything about business'. Remember this, nothing beats hard work, integrity, people skills, sales skills and the desire to take a risk or two to turn it all into reality.

This clearly brings us to the fourth (and by far the most challenging) belief most employees struggle with: The security of the steady paycheck.

What's more secure … a business with one customer who buys everything you produce, or a business with tens of thousands of customers who each buy a small portion of what you produce, and who keep coming back to buy more.

Of course it's not the one with a single customer. The JOB, with just one boss, even though it feels like it's more secure, is not.

One of the biggest challenges I have when working with Level 0 Employees is they make their decisions based on fear, on what could go wrong, rather than on vision, trust, and on what can go right.

Fear, in almost all cases, is the one thing stopping people making the leap from Level 0 to Level 1 and beyond.

This introduces the reason for fear, or belief number five on our hit list: 'I don't know enough to start my own business'.

Jumping from Level 0 into the world of business requires a fundamental shift in thinking. It requires a shift from a thought process of fear to a thought process of trust.

Trust in yourself.

Trusting you'll learn along the way, trusting you'll make mistakes, but that you can recover. Trusting the only way to truly learn how to be an entrepreneur is to just get started.

Remember, fear of the unknown is natural. But, living a life without the courage to step through your fears is un-natural.

All greatness follows a leap of faith, a courageous step into the unknown, into a world of new things, new challenges and new possibilities.

Understand this; anyone can make the jump from Level 0 to Level 1. It takes courage, trust and self-belief. It also takes ACTION.


**An Employee's Relationship with Money**

At each of the five levels we're going to examine a relationship with money. I like to think of money as having a personality, of having a way of being, and our relationship with it/him/her/them, determines its relationship with us.

By the way, we're also going to find out each level's 'word' that describes that level's association with money.

Let's consider Level 0 …

How does an employee relate to money? Yes, I know they think of it as scarce, that there never seems to be enough in most cases, but I'm looking deeper.

What is the one word employees use to determine their ability to bring in money. That's right, they EARN money.

So, what's the definition of 'earn'?

The dictionary defines it this way: 'To get in return for work.'

I'd put it even simpler ... earn is a verb, or as I learnt in grade 3 ... a DOING word. It's a word that needs both time spent and physical exertion to make it happen.

With this one simple word we get a very clear understanding of how an employee's world is so defined by what they DO. The very definition of the word 'employee' makes it ever so clear. Once again my dictionary states: 'A person employed for wages.'

With such a definition of yourself, how else would you ever be able to assume anything other than the fact you should work hard, get promoted and EARN as much as you can.

## Reasons to be an Employee

I know it seems like I've been giving employees a hard time, and rightly so, I have been. But, there are some extremely good arguments for being an employee for a certain period of your life.

Despite this fact, most people won't give you the reasons I'll show you below, and not because they're so obscure, but because most people arguing this point are employees and are thus, by virtue of their lack of experience, limited in their entrepreneurial thinking.

As an entrepreneur, you'll realize there are two very good reasons why I'd suggest most people who are starting out financially get themselves a job.

The first reason is to build CAPITAL.

Not to buy things, nor to live the high life, but to save, to put away and to keep their income well invested in order to build up working and purchasing capital for their first few businesses and properties.

When most people first want to go into business for themselves, they usually realize although they have the skills to do it, they still can't. Why? Because they've spent all of their income on STUFF.

So, Rule Number One for the employee is ... build capital.

That rule is just as important as Rule Number Two... building knowledge.

Consider this: A friend wanted to get into the restaurant business recently. My advice to him was to go and work in someone else's restaurant first.

Why, you may ask?

So he could get experience, learn, make mistakes in someone else's business and not his own, and most importantly to build knowledge so he would know what to look for when the time came for him to buy his own restaurant.

These, in my opinion, are the only two reasons to get yourself a job. Does                                    this mean I am suggesting you quit the job you have right now, if you have one? Well, yes and no ...

The job has to always meet both criteria. Can you learn from the job you have now, and can you build capital from the job you have right now?

One last point here. I personally believe it's far more important for a job to teach you something than it is for it to finance you. These lessons will set you up for life, whereas the money will generally not last that long.

So, get a job where your boss is a great mentor, or where your boss does everything wrong so that you can learn how NOT to do it. But whatever you do, get a job that teaches you first and pays you second.

## Security and THE System

Think back to THE System I mentioned in the first chapter. The system of schooling, bankers, media, government, religion and employment that teaches you to get a good job, buy a house on a mortgage, pay taxes and interest all your life, buy lots of STUFF and have just enough left over to get by on. Then you can retire at 65 as a good employee and live the good life.

Think about what having to make mortgage payments, car payments, credit card payments, school payments, and all other payments every single month means. You've already committed yourself to spending, in most cases, hundreds or thousands of dollars before the month even starts.

No wonder employees have a fear of not getting any money next month. They're already in a negative cashflow situation before the month starts.

That's why you have to take on the first financial challenge in life of building enough PASSIVE income through your investments to cover your monthly expenses. That way you're really stepping into the realm of the financially secure.

I know if you had money coming in you'd feel secure. You'd not have to worry about where the money was coming from if you were to start your own business. But each and every employee has to break their addiction to the paycheck somewhere in order to break their addiction to security so they can reach freedom.

## Moving Up from Employee

Maybe it'll take having a husband or wife with a salary for most employees to jump into business for themselves. Maybe they'll wait until they're into their 40's or 50's when they've built up a level of wealth and their kids have left home.

My recommendation is get into the game of business as soon as you can. As you read through the next few chapters (as well as my other books and those on my recommended reading list) you'll learn what it takes to get into business, stay in business and become rich through business.

All I can say is this …

Courage means having fear and doubt, but taking action anyway. If you're one of the top 1% of the top 1% of employees in the world you'll get wealthy that way. Just remember these two facts though when you're faced with the decision of whether to get into business or not: The majority of millionaires are business owners, and "When is NOW ever a good time to get started?"

## Level 1 – The Self-Employed

This is usually the first jump on the entrepreneurial ladder and for most, it's the only jump. In fact, most entrepreneurs never seem to get past this level of growth in their business.

The truth is you really can't call it a business; you've really got to call it a JOB. And of course you do remember what J.O.B. stands for, don't you? Just Over Broke.

What's more, this job is most probably one of the worst jobs in the world. I think it's put best by this quote, taken from one of my live seminars: "Most people thought they worked for an idiot BEFORE they started their own business."

I really don't think most people who start their own business know what they're getting themselves into. In fact, most look at it as something glamorous, exciting, and with such a sense of new found freedom they're fooled into believing wealth is just a few days, weeks or months away.

To become self-employed, what usually happens is one of two things...

EITHER ... you're unemployed and looking for a new job when one morning you have what I call a Blinding Flash of the Obvious.

"I know," you say, "I'll start my own business. Then no one will ever be able to fire me."

And with all of the planning of the team that built and sailed the Titanic you get started.

OR ... you're working for someone else and you keep thinking these three things to yourself:

"I can do a better job than them?"

"How come they get ALL the money, when I do all the work?" and,

"If I owned this company, I'd be the boss, I'd make everyone else do the work, I'd play golf, relax, and I'd work a lot less."

Either way, there is one thing running through the mind of every single man or woman as they jump into the role of the Self-Employed Entrepreneur …

"I'm going to be the boss …"

And with that the race starts.

It's one of the biggest steps you'll ever take, and believe me, the most rewarding you'll ever choose, so if you've taken it, that's great. Learn about how to step up further. If not, get ready to learn how to make it work for you …

## The Entrepreneurial Mindset of the Self-Employed

You see, while the emotional driving force behind most employees is security, those who step into the role of the self-employed are driven by another emotional factor.

This is the desire to be in CONTROL of their own life, and of their own destiny.

And, armed with this desire and marching to their theme song, Frank Sinatra's, 'I did it MY way' they're off to create something they never expected.

They're going to create a job.

A self-employed person starts out with just one employee; himself or herself. And that suits them fine; no one else to worry about, none of those other people who make all the mistakes, it's just them.

The self-employed person usually trusts no one other than themself to get the job done.

They'll say things like: "I am my business." Or, in their sales pitch: "You'll be dealing directly with me and I'm the owner of the business". Or, "If you want something done right, you've got to do it yourself." Or, "Everything is under my control so I know that it's done right".

Remember, most self-employed people started their own business because they thought they were so good at what they did, or so good at making what they sell, they mistakenly assumed they could run a business that sells what they make or do.

This mindset of being the eternally great employee was fantastic when you worked for someone else, but as you'll soon see, it's the fastest way to hard work, and often bankruptcy, as a business owner.

Starting a business where you are an expert at what the business does is usually the first and biggest mistake made by the majority of people going into business.

They start a business in which they know how to make what the business sells, instead of starting, or buying, a business in which they know how to sell what the business makes.

This is the start of the self-employed trap.

If you can do what the business does, and especially if you're the best at it, then it's almost a sure thing you're going to be trapped doing that work forever and a day.

Now, while the trap has already been set, it's this second factor that usually ensures every self-employed person falls into it.

Not only do they desire control, and think that no one is as good as they are but … they don't have a VISION of 'doing' anything else.

In general, their entire vision is limited by their previous training as a Level 0 Employee. They've never been trained when you set up a company, you have to start with the end in mind.

You have to start it knowing what you're doing is creating something that'll work without you. More about the specifics of this as we go on, but first, let's look at making your Vision break-through.

What Entrepreneurs know that most Self-Employed are yet to learn is how to envision in their mind and then put on paper what they see as the future of the business.

The Self-Employed are trapped by the limited 'doing' vision that is a part of being an employee. As an example, computer technicians who starts their own businesses usually sees themselves servicing people's computers and would be extremely happy if they could get enough business to keep themselves, and only themselves, extremely busy.

In other words, most Level 1 Self-Employed people want to be BUSY. They seem to think that business is spelt – BUSYness. In a moment I'm going to introduce you to the see-saw effect that means very few will ever reach the point where they're always busy making money, and thus they're almost always frustrated.

Now don't get me wrong. By accident, some will break through this trap all on their own, BUT most are truly set to stay right here until they reach a point of frustration - a frustration that leads to more than 80% of Level 1 Self-Employed people calling it quits.

They say: "It's not worth all the trouble. I'm going back to get a job and work for someone else."

So, before you make the same mistake, let's examine this Vision thing.

When you go into business you need to create a vision that not only sees the business working without you, but one that will inspire and enrol the people who'll be joining your team. You need to be able to see your business as more than just yourself.

You need to see it as a true business, and NOT just as a job for yourself.

You need to create a Vision of YOU being more than just a worker in your own business - more than just a manager in your own business. You need to create a Vision of a business that works without you ... in other words, an investment, your investment.

More about this as we get into the next few levels of entrepreneurs.

### The Self-Employed's Relationship with Money

Almost an extension of the mindset challenges we've just looked at, most Level 1 Self-Employed people's relationship with money needs to be examined.

As you may or may not know, the way you relate to money will determine your financial future. And, given you've only got one shot at this thing called life, let's make sure you give it the best shot you can.

A Level 1 has a very similar relationship to money as that of the Level 0 Employee. Remember the employee's word was 'EARN', a verb or DO'ing word.

With the Self Employed, the word changes but the DO'ing-ness remains the same. They're still trading time for money. And their word in relation to bringing in money is now, MAKE.

They have to 'MAKE' money in their business.

The dictionary definition of 'make' is: 'To bring into existence, especially by effort.'

So by definition, with this relationship to money you're still going to be working hard for every dollar you get. You're still trading time for money. Yes, you may be getting more dollars for each hour you work, but the see-saw the Self-Employed ride never lets them truly create financial freedom. More on that in a moment.

Whilst we're on definitions, here's the definition for 'Self': 'Person's nature, special qualities, one's own personality.'

And the definition for 'Employed': 'Give work to, usually for payment.'

Once again by definition you've positioned yourself in a place that from a true Entrepreneurs viewpoint is not only guaranteed to mean physical involvement in your money making activities, but also that there's very little difference to being employed by someone else.

The only real difference is now you have the headaches of being both an employee and an employer.

Yet I want you to remember this: Getting to Level 1 – Self-Employed is the first step up the ladder of financial freedom, and those who have taken it are usually far closer to becoming financially free than those who never leave Level 0.

So, congratulations if you have, and congratulations in advance if you're about to …

## Reasons for being Self-Employed

There are at least eight very powerful reasons for being Self-Employed. Reasons that simply put are a must if you're at all serious about getting yourself into the ranks of the RICH …

Remember back to Level 0, employees have absolutely no true leverage; they're simply trading time for dollars. We'll get to the benefits of moving up to Level 1 – Self-Employed shortly, but just keep this in mind:

When you're selling for yourself, there's no set hourly rate … you, through your skills, your level of work and your passion or determination, are able to determine your level of income. No one else can make that decision for a Self-Employed person. And, whilst that scares some, it feels great to the many who take this step.

In fact, that level of self-control promised by the 'I did it my way' feeling is central to the decision most people make when becoming Self-Employed. And whilst being your own boss, and the ability to determine your own hours and income, are seen as the main reasons why anyone would choose to step up to Level 1 – Self Employed, they are not the reasons I would give you to make this step …

So, my reasons for becoming a Level 1 – Self-Employed person.

Most of my reasons for becoming a Self-Employed moneymaker have to do with what you'll learn along the way. Hopefully, you'll already have mastered a few of these areas as an Employee and thus your time as a Self-Employed person will be a short stint as you race up the ladder.

Reason 1 … You'll have to learn about company structure and set-up. You'll probably also need to understand the difference between a holding company and a trading company. Why you should always have two companies rather than one: one to own the assets, the other to trade and make the on-going profits.

Reason 2 … You'll also need to learn accounting, bookkeeping and how to interact with your accountant. You may, for the first time in your life, get yourself an accountant.

Knowing where to look for the answers to your questions about the Balance Sheet, the Profit and Loss Statement, the Cashflow or any Budgets you do is a must if you're ever to move up the ladder.

Whilst accounting is a background part of day-to-day business, it's like the engine room. Without it you may as well be playing sport and not keeping score …

Reason 3 … and probably the most important two things you'll ever learn at Level 1, if you didn't already as a Level 0, is sales and marketing.

Becoming a great salesperson is a must if you're going to sell a lot both in your first business and in any business you start or buy in the future. Sales means everything from face-to-face, over the phone, cold calling and even getting over any fear you have of talking to people. Sales also mean doing presentations to groups and selling to more than one person at a time.

It's easy to say, but becoming great at sales requires a lot of reading, learning and application. It may even take you a few years if you've never done it before as an Employee

And marketing, well what can I say that hasn't already been said. Together with sales, it's the lifeblood of any business. A true Entrepreneur knows while cost reduction is important, bringing in the cashflow is by far the most important area for any company.

You can cut costs to profit, but you can only sell your way to prosperity. Whilst 'sales' is the ability to turn a lead into a sale, 'marketing' is the ability to generate prospects at a reasonable price. Read two of my other books, Instant Cashflow and Cash, Customers, and Ads that Sell to make sure you know the best marketing information there is.

Now, let's look at Reason 4 … as a new business owner, you get the privilege of doing everything yourself, and one thing you really get to learn is the meaning of Hard Work. You'll often complete 16 and 20-hour days, six or seven days a week.

Not because there is just so much work to do, but because you're having fun, you're learning, growing and most of all, because you're working out how to design a business as you go along. Growing a business is like riding a bike: once you've done it a few times, it gets really easy.

Think of all the extra work as your entrepreneurial apprenticeship and study being done after hours …

Reason 5 … one of the most important lessons every new business owner learns is Cost Reductions. As a Self-Employed Level 1 Entrepreneur, you'll be forced to scrimp and save, to recycle, to borrow, to use old second-hand stuff and to do whatever it takes to get by.

Once again, whilst it's most important for a company to bring in money, lack of control over your costs is a certain death knock for a small business. Learning this 'tight' way of doing business is great; you'll need to remember it, especially as you get bigger.

Reason 6 … for becoming Self-Employed is to simply Make Contacts. The bigger your people network, the easier you'll find it to do business, any business. Or, to put it another way, join as many networking groups as you can, go to as many seminars as you can, to not only learn, but to get yourself out there meeting other business people.

In business, the old axiom of 'who you know' is extremely important, so learn to meet lots of people.

Reason 7 … As a Self-Employed Level 1, you'll also have to relearn the meaning of Responsibility and Accountability. Nowhere else is it as important to learn these virtues than as the boss of your own company. The 'buck' really does start and stop with you.

Far too often the world of the Level 0 Employee is littered with 'pass the buck' people. When these people start or buy there own business, it's almost certain they'll fail. Only those with the passion and desire to lead a life of total ownership will ever succeed in their own business.

Of course, another great reason (Reason 8) for becoming Self-Employed is to Make More Money. Usually a good employee will make a whole lot more money as a Self-Employed business owner. This is not just because they're making more, but because of all the appropriate and legal tax deductions they can claim, the fact they pay tax only on their profits and not on their entire wage, and they pay tax at the end, and not at the beginning, like an Employee would.

To top it all off, people seem to work harder when they know the dollars are going into their own pocket and not someone else's.

And the Ninth most important reason is so you at least start to learn technology.  Hopefully like many others you learnt these lessons at someone else's expense as an employee, but if not, prepare for a lot of learning and growth as you get your first company up and running at a profit.

Technology is here to stay and it's a painful business life for anyone who decides not to make it an integral part of his or her knowledge base.

To finish off … whilst most think the reasons for becoming self-employed are to take control and to be the boss, the exact opposite is true for the serious Entrepreneur …

Start your small business now, even if it's part-time, to gain the knowledge you'll need in a few years time when you're playing with big dollars and running your big businesses …

## The See-Saw of being Self-Employed

As I mentioned, as a Level 1 Self-Employed person, your business life will feel just like a see-saw.  While it's often true a Level 1 can make more per hour than they ever could as an Employee, the challenge comes down to how many hours are actually used in the background.

You'll spend half your life chasing the work doing Marketing, Sales and Administration and then you'll have so much work to do you'll have to flip over and start doing the work …

Doing the Work is one side of the see-saw and Sales and Marketing is the other.

Chase the work, do the work, chase the work, do the work, chase the work, do the work … and so on …

It's this see-saw that stops a Self-Employed Entrepreneur ever really getting ahead. Once again, you're still in a situation where there's no real leverage. You still need to DO the work.

It's also this see-saw that gets Level 1 Self-Employed people to make one of two decisions. To either give it up and go back and get a job, or to take the plunge and jump in the deep end of business and make the decision to grow their business, to move up the ladder …

## Moving Up from Self-Employed

The first step in getting yourself up the ladder is 'Your Vision'. As long as you can only ever see yourself running a one-person business, you'll never be anything more.

You've got to build a Vision of a big business, a business that needs to be big to achieve the Vision you set. Maybe your Vision is to change the world, to change your industry or to be the best in your industry. Whatever your Vision, the bigger it is, the bigger your business needs to become to complete it.

Set a Vision of what your business will be like when you've finished building it. You see, you have to plan it from the start so at some stage in the near future, your business will run without you. Plan for it from the beginning.

Whilst we're on change, one of the most important changes you'll need to make is your Identity. You'll have to stop thinking of yourself as a worker and start thinking of yourself as a business owner.

For example, you may need to stop thinking of yourself as a plumber and become the owner of a plumbing business, an entrepreneur who's currently building a plumbing business. Or, you may have to remember to stop telling people you're a hairdresser and start thinking of yourself as the owner of a growing hairdressing empire.

One other thing here, stop thinking of yourself or your business as being SMALL … calling yourself a small business is extremely limiting. You can be a growth business, a prototype business or even think of yourself as a big business. Don't just change your own Identity, change the Identity of your business as well,

I know this all seems overly simplistic, and it could even be just a mind game, but it's by far the most important step you need to take on your climb up the 5 Levels of Entrepreneurship. Set your Vision as soon as you can.

Next step you need to take is to change your Goals …

Set larger goals, much larger goals, ask for more and then be prepared to get it. There's nothing worse than the limits you place upon yourself by setting small goals. Goals that may at the time seem a stretch in reality might just get you to work a little harder.

You see, when you set goals that are entirely massive compared with your current results, it challenges you to think entirely differently, to do things entirely differently, and that in itself is essentially what this growth process is all about.

Once you've created your new Vision, new Identity and your new, much larger and more inspiring Goals, it's time to get to work ON the business.

Firstly, you'll need to establish your very own Position Chart. That is, a chart of all the different jobs there will be in your company when it's finished. Not the people, the jobs.

This may take a little thought as to how many different jobs you do each day right now, but eventually it will become very clear exactly what it is you're building.

The moment you're clear on what your business needs to look like when it's finished, you're well on track to making it happen.

From here, you'll need to create Position Statements for each and every position in your company. Write down and get clear on who does what by when. Flowchart how sales and orders and paperwork move through your company so everyone can see where they fit into the picture.

Then, when you are completely clear on what each and every position within the company does, you can allocate people into every position on the chart. At the start YOU will be in every box and have to complete every position. You'll also need to allocate Key Performance Indicators (KPI's) for each position so you can see if they're doing their job well from a small set of numbers.

Read Michael Gerber's book The E-Myth Revisited if you want to learn a little more about this.

Now that you're here, it's time to fill the positions. I always start by filling the positions I'm spending most of my time on right now. This might be sales and marketing, delivery, customer service, manufacturing, or any other group of positions within your business.

Remember these few tips when going into the recruitment and hiring of people. Learn the **ACTION International** Recruitment System from either the Competitive Edge Audio Tapes or from you nearest **ACTION** Coach. You should hire people based on their heart and spirit first and on their mind and body skill-set second. Make sure you hire people who can fill as many boxes as possible when you first start hiring. And lastly, don't just hire someone because they're available, hire only someone you're really excited about hiring, someone who'll be a star performer.

By the way, many people ask me the question: "When am I big enough to put someone on?" My suggestion is you hire when you are making enough to afford half of their wages. They will make you enough to pay for at least the other half.

So, last but not least, we face the question: "Why should I grow past Level 1 – Self-Employed?"  Why indeed …

You can safely stay here making a good level of income and a reasonable lifestyle.  You can work in your own business every day for the rest of time until you decide to retire … and yet …

You've read this far, you've committed to getting yourself to a level of wealth that the time commitments of Level 1 – Self-Employed cannot give you.  Level 1 starts your education, it starts your ability to get yourself a high level of income, but remember, income is not wealth and wealth is not RICH …

So, let's take the next step to getting rich …

## Level 2 – The Manager

So, you've made the leap …

Now you've got employees and if you're like most people in this situation, you think all of your dreams are about to come true … you'll finally be able to work less, start making a whole lot more and life will be just great.

Again, also if you're like most people, nothing could be further from the truth.  You're working harder, longer hours, doing your own work and fixing up the mistakes of everyone around you, you're probably making no more than before, or even a little less, and as the old saying goes … 'this looks nothing like the brochure' …

So, let's take a couple of steps back so we can make hundreds forward. Hopefully you learnt a lot by understanding how to move from a Level 1 – Self-Employed with the Vision, Identity, Goals, Position Chart, Position Statements, Key Performance Indicators and the Recruitment System.

You see, I imagine because the company was growing you went out and just had to employ someone to give you a hand. Of course, you gave them all the jobs you hated and most probably you hired a friend of a friend because they were out of work.

HINT: There is probably a very sound reason they were out of work!

Growing a business past Level 1 into a Successful Level 2 isn't an easy task; if it were everyone would do it. In fact, as you already know, most Level 1's decide to go back and get a job and most Level 2 Managers eventually decide to sack everyone and go back to when it was just them. That is, go back to Level 1.

Hopefully, we'll save you all that anguish ...

You see, growth brings about it's own set of challenges, and as I've said before, the hardest business to build is your first one because you have to learn as you grow. CASHFLOW management is one of the biggest challenges growth brings, not to mention team building, systems and leadership ...

One of the biggest traps of reaching Level 2 – Manager, and staying there, is arriving at the thought: "I've made it ..."

The moment you think you've made it, be aware this is, in reality, the first step on the path to your business getting ready for a fall. So, why does this happen over and over again? Because too many business owners who are making good money, get sick of working and want to walk away before they've 'finished' the business; before it's ready to run without them.

And this, my friend, is one of the fastest ways to kill your cashflow machine.

**The Entrepreneurial Mindset of The Manager**

Most people who get stuck at the Manager level are prone to a set of beliefs about business that are truly the only thing standing in the way of their success.

Firstly, let's deal with the total mistaken business belief 'Bigger is Better'. For some insane reason it's become a socially accepted belief the bigger you grow your business the better it will be. Along the same lines it's thought by some the way to solve all your business woes is to just get bigger.

How wrong can two assumptions be! It's kind of like motivating idiots; they just do stupid things faster.

Growing bigger when you're running a business that demands you being there all day, every day, is just plain lunacy. If you found it hard to cope with the mistakes and errors when you dealt with 20 customers each day, what do you think you'll inherit with 200 customers per day?

I've seen so many companies grow themselves to death; it's not funny. Growing so fast, robbing Peter to pay Paul, and all the while their mistakes and lack of profitability is covered over by their rate of growth and the extra people they employ.

These companies seem to survive, although, no one really knows how or why. Many then fall into the trap of the second belief … More Employee's means More Successful …

Once again this is a completely crazy scenario. So much so I laugh when I hear someone bragging about how many people they employ. They seem to think because they pay a huge wages bill each month they must be more successful than the rest of us.

Not so. All this means is rather than turning to a better solution to run their business, they've turned to an older outdated solution called 'hire more people'. If only they'd realized business has nothing to do with how many people you employ and everything to do with how much money you make.

Oh, that reminds me ... NOT ... More Revenue means More Successful ...

Oh no, this is another beautiful example of ego overriding brain power, logic and common sense, just to name a few.

Now admittedly your total revenues can determine your company's value, but nowhere near the extent that profits can.

If only they'd realize bigger is not better and stop growing for the sake of growing, they might realize profit is the only score that really counts.

One last belief the Level 2 Managers seem to have found for themselves. They truly believe that ... 'Nobody's as Good as Me'.

And what's more, in most cases it's true.

Why? Not because the employees, or as I call them - team members, can't be as good, but because the Manager is a really bad leader.

In most cases, the employees have had bad training, bad goal setting, bad everything and most importantly, no-where near enough experience.

Managers hire people they can control rather than people they can lead.

I think it was Henry Ford who said: "The smartest people in the world hire people smarter than themselves."

However, the Manager seems to have a firm belief: 'If you want the job done right, you've got to do it yourself'.

All because they want to be the boss and feel super important.

Probably the biggest ego trip of all for Level 2 Managers is of being the boss. Our Level 1 friends sang along with Frank Sinatra, yet our Level 2 buddys have no theme song ...

Just a firm desire to be Bruce Springsteen ... The Boss ...

They seem to love the power of being in charge more than they love the profits, more than watching others succeed, more than seeing a manual task completed and much more than going home early and trusting other people to do a great job.

Now of course those still stuck at Level 2 will be reading this and feeling ready to kill me, or at least they will totally refute everything I've said, and with good reason (excuses) as to why their situation is different. And yes, it is different; but they now have the choice to change.

By the way, one last belief you'll have to remove if you really want to move and grow: The old 'I just can't get good people' belief.

I remember saying this to my Dad when I was 21. He replied very bluntly, as he so often did: "Brad, you're getting the people you deserve."

It took me quite some time to calm down and realize what he said was a simple truth. When I started running a great company I'd get great people, and when I became a great leader, I started running a great company.

I know this all seems so simple, but often the most profound ideas are the simplest. Become a great leader, you'll get great people and they'll run the business for you …

## The Manager's Relationship with Money

Once again it's time to examine the relationship you may have with money as a Level 2 - Manager.

The first and foremost belief that has stayed with them is from their days as an employee. They still believe in the tradition of having to Work Hard to Make a Living.

Notice it doesn't say anything about working smart to get RICH …

Let's re-examine how this belief gets to stick in their minds and how we can remove it. Remember back to when you were first taught to work hard, probably by a parent or a leadership figure in your life. You probably even thought it made sense ... work hard = big rewards ...

The problem was no one ever defined what type of work you should be doing the hardest ...

Einstein was once quoted as saying: "Thinking is the hardest work, that's why so few engage in it."

This brings us back to our word for money ...

At Level 2 - Manager, it's still 'Make', and by definition we remember that as meaning: 'Construct or produce by combining parts or putting materials together.'

By definition then, we're clearly DEFINED, once again, into our role.

By the way, the definition for manager is: 'A person who controls a business'.

It has always become clear, after we've had it pointed out a Manager is there to manage resources and a Leader is there to lead people, that most Level 2's are trying to CONTROL their STAFF rather than LEAD their TEAM.

This simple belief is a high predictor of the Level 2 Manager's ability to only draw a wage from their business and generally never a profit of any real worth ...

That's compounded by their last major Level 2 money relationship factor; that the 'Company's Money is My Money'. Unfortunately most Level 2's are still finding it hard to distinguish between their own money and the company's money.

They refer to money the company made as 'I or We Made' rather than referring to the profit they received. This one simple split of reference to the company as an investment as well as a job, can make a major difference to the way you go about building your income, your wealth, and your company …

Overall it's pretty simple to see Level 2 Managers are almost the same as the Level 1 Self-Employed, only now they have a few more headaches, a few more people to chase after and a few more bills to pay. Yet one thing still remains the same, they still have to go to work if they want to make any money …

They still associate money with the Verb, or doing word … MAKE …

## Reasons to be The Manager

I know it seems like I'm beating up on everyone at the Manager level, and yes it's true - I am. But, there are some truly valid reasons to be the Level 2 Manager.

Remember, although your first business will involve the most work because you're learning along the way … it will only get easier.

So, here's what you should learn, and therefore get value from, at Level 2 – Manager …

You'll have to learn Team Building - a very intricate subject and most probably the toughest one at this level, but to progress you'll have to have a great team who can run your business without you.

You'll get to learn about Systems and how to get them to run your business for you. You see Systems should run a business and People should run the Systems. This simple statement can turn into 12 months solid work for even the most professional systems writer, or years for a first time rookie business owner, unless of course you learn a better way.

Most business owners never, ever learn this lesson of Systems and thus the business will always depend upon them being there. Go to www.actionplanning.tv and you'll see our AutoPilot Program and how easy it can be to systemize your business.

Next, you'll have to learn Delegation and Trust. You can't build a great team without it and no systems will work unless you let them.

You'll have to learn how to handle Growth. Cashflow, supplies and so on all become a factor here. Many books have been written about this and yes ... you will have to read at least one book on each.

Now are you starting to see why very few people pass this test? Stepping up from Manager requires the greatest level of self-belief and learning of all the Steps.

There's still more to learn. You'll get to learn about Building Relationships with your Bankers and Suppliers. This alone will allow so much more growth than you can imagine in your business.

You'll get to learn Resource Allocation, either re-actively through a big mistake (what I call a learning experience) or pro-actively through study and asking the right questions of the best people. Remember, you manage resources, and you lead people ...

This one is high on your list; you'll have to learn Quick Decision Making. The faster and bigger your business grows, the better your decisions will need to become. And better decisions come from better-educated questions ...you'll learn Accountability ... This is about the next step up from responsibility. At Responsibility it's about you and your immediate results and actions. At Accountability it's about your whole team and their results and actions.

Probably the biggest mind stretch is to learn Juggling. You'll need to have at least a dozen thoughts running through your head at any one point in time.  Once again though, the bigger you get, the more you'll have to juggle.

And last but not least, probably one of the more exciting reasons to go through Level 2 – Manager is so that you can … Make More Money.

At every stage of business the level of your personal income should grow substantially.  If it doesn't, you're doing something wrong, massively wrong …

Go back and re-read this section if you're at Level 2 – Manager and you're income is shrinking, or contact your nearest **ACTION** Coach … there is obviously something you've missed.

## Working Hard and Getting Nowhere

Almost anyone who's either been through Level 2 – Manager, or is currently stuck at Level 2, will tell you it seems like a whole lot of work to get nowhere. You see, growth brings with it it's own set of challenges. There never seems to be enough time in the day to get anything done. The phone never seems to stop ringing and your staff pester you incessantly. You seem to be going round and round in circles. You're spending 80% of your time on day-to-day matters and 20% on developing systems that will run your business. On top of that, there are customers to deal with as well as reps from other businesses. You can't remember when you last had a lunch break.

You probably think back to your days as a Level 1 – Self-Employed with fondness and deduce that all you've scored by moving up a rung on the ladder I call The Five Levels of Entrepreneurship is Double the Trouble.

Level 2 Managers certainly become very good at Putting Out Fires. Remember I mentioned your need to develop the ability for Quick Decision Making?  The faster and bigger your business grows, the better your decisions will need to become - especially as you will be juggling many things at the same time. Businesses are confronted with numerous problems - business problems, financial problems, marketing problems, staffing problems – each and every day. To survive and prosper, you will need to make the right decisions most of the time. And you will need to make them fast.

Many Level 2 Managers begin to wonder if all they are working for is their employees. But remember I said probably the toughest and most intricate subject you'll have to master before moving on to Level 3 is Team Building. It may seem all you are working for is your employees, but as long as you are doing all the things necessary to build a great team, one that can run your business without you, then you're well on your way to the next level, and to RICHES.

Here's another thing many of you might identify with: 'Where's all the Profit gone?' Well, at least you are thinking in terms of PROFIT. It's a sad fact most Level 2 Managers generally never benefit from a profit of any real worth.

You may be wondering whether you're making any progress at this level. You never seem to have any time on your hands, and even though you're no longer doing all the work yourself, you spend all your time running around in circles. The funny thing about being a Manager is you think all the people you've hired work for you. You end up working for them; chasing after them, fixing up all their mistakes and taking over their problems. You're also probably paying them more than you pay yourself. Understand this; you may not be earning massive amounts here, but as long as your learning, that's OK.

**Moving Up from The Manager**

So how do you break the 'working hard and getting nowhere' cycle? What do you need to do to progress up the ladder to Level 3?

Let's start by exploring why people get stuck at this level. They can't progress up the ladder to Level 3 because they didn't learn everything they should have at Level 1, and at Level 2, they should have been learning everything they could about things like systems, team building, leadership, human resources, and recruitment instead of running around in circles after their people.

If you want to avoid these pitfalls, you desperately need a good system in your business. Systems are required for a very good reason – not just because it's fashionable for growing businesses to have them, but because they allow the business to function smoothly, sharing out the workload according to the skills and talents of all members of the team. And more importantly, a system allows you to get on with the task of managing.

Now once you have reached the point where you have implemented a system and consequently begun to manage effectively, you will be able to concentrate on providing meaningful leadership. One spin-off of sound leadership is it results in better team building, which in turn will assist you in providing effective leadership once more. It's a classic chicken and egg situation.

Remember, these are two of the major challenges facing every Level 2 Manager. But get them right, and you will be one huge step closer to your ultimate goal of building a business that will produce profits, even without you.

You can't grow a business without good people, but how many times have you heard someone say they just can't get good people. Understand that you only get the people you deserve. If you're not a good leader, you won't get good people. The moment you become a good leader, you'll get good people. The moment you start running a good business, you'll get good customers.

Every sizeable organization requires a leader – that goes without saying. But as your organization grows – and it will if you are following these basic strategies – you will find you need more than one leader. Each specialist area will need its own leader. In this way you need a Financial Manager, a Manufacturing Manager, a Marketing Manager, a Sales Manager and an Administration Manager. You get my point. Once this happens, you will need to start thinking about appointing a General Manager or even a President. You might decide to fill this position yourself initially, but eventually you will see  the advantages of moving up the ladder.

At this stage, you may, like many, question the need to move up.

Many business owners in this position simply decide to stay put, for various reasons. They may be happy operating at this level. They may not have the vision of growing.

Level 1 may well have started your education and it may have given you a higher income than you were earning as an employee. But at Level 2, you will be setting the foundations for further growth.

You need to ensure you have learnt about, and  mastered, the art of team building; you must get to grips with systems and how to develop them. You also need to learn how to handle growth, how to delegate and how to develop trust.  Relationship building, resource allocation, juggling and decision making will by now be skills you will be using on a daily basis.

The end result is you will be managing in an accountable and responsible manner.

You will also be itching to get rich…

# Level 3 – The Owner/Leader

By now you will have realized trading time for money is NOT the formula for getting rich.

You will have also realized, until now, that's basically what you were doing.

Now I know you will have been gaining all sorts of necessary skills along the way that are essential for the move up to Level 3, but if you think about it, until now you have really been nothing more than a glorified employee.

Understand this: the move from Level 2 to Level 3 requires a mindset change, especially when it comes to the way you relate to money.

When you moved up from Level 2, you've really moved out of the position of having a JOB – you are now SEMI-RETIRED. Instead of just making money by taking a wage from the business, you've started to get PROFIT. Very few people ever reach Level 3, and of those that do, most get there by accident. They tend to stay at this level running their businesses, probably because they never get over the need to feel wanted.

At the level of Owner/Leader, you need to learn to let go. Your relationship with your business will be a whole lot different. You'll most probably lean back in your chair, sigh, and say: "I've made it! I'm here at last and this is fun."

Let me point out something here before we go on any further. It's usually at this stage that Owner/Leader stops forging ahead. This is extremely dangerous because if a business stops growing, it begins dying. It's no different from a tree. If a tree isn't growing, it's dying. It's as simple as that.

As an Owner/Leader you'll also have a whole lot more time on your hands than you've ever had before – and you won't be used to it. And for good reason; you see, as an Owner/Leader you'll have three things going for you that Managers don't. You'll have good SYSTEMS in place so your people can get on with the job without you having to be there. You'll have built a TEAM instead of simply having a bunch of employees. And you'll have appointed a GENERAL MANAGER.

Of course, there's another very important thing you will have learnt to get to this level, and that's to TRUST.

You'll also be spending a whole lot more. You see, because you'll be thinking: "No one needs me around here anymore," you'll step in and change things. You'll most probably invest in new technology, upgrade the office, and buy more office furniture, that sort of thing. You'll be thinking very differently now to when you were a Level 2 Manager.

And most importantly, you'll be a true manager, working in the background where necessary, giving encouragement and guidance to your team. You'll also be letting them take the credit for their successes, and you'll be directing the course of the business as it grows and prospers.

**The Entrepreneurial Mindset of The Owner/Leader**

Owner/Leaders experience a massive mindset shift when they first move up to this level. They operate on an entirely different level to the Manager.

Their relationship to the business is entirely different for a start. This brings with it a different way of doing things.

As an Owner/Leader, one of the first most important attributes you will have is that you receive passive income. You've reached the position where it doesn't matter whether you get out of bed or not each day. The business can carry on without you having to be there.

You see, you have progressed from working IN the business to working ON the business and now you can relax. This might take some getting used to, especially as you're so used to doing things yourself because nobody could do it as good as you could.

As an Owner/Leader you're NOT a hands-on person. This means you'll take a more holistic view of the business. You'll be operating at the strategic level and concentrating on the big picture. Your focus is no longer on CASHFLOW (others do that now), but on PROFIT. The question you'll ask most often is: "Where's the Profit?"

## The Owner/Leaders Relationship with Money

Once again it's time to examine the relationship you may have with money as a Level 3 - Owner/Leader.

As an Owner/Leader you've moved into semi-retirement, and as a result, you no longer trade time for income. You work SMARTER, and get RICHER…

This means there is no longer a requirement for personal exertion. Your level of income is no longer a function of the amount of effort you put in, or of the amount of time you spend working. Your income is now rather a function of the level of PROFIT the business makes.

Let's stop there for a moment and examine the word 'Owner'. Again, we will turn to the dictionary for guidance. An owner is defined as: 'A person who owns something.' Pretty straight forward, don't you think? And if we look at the verb 'Own', we find the dictionary describes it as: 'possess; have as property.'

What then of the word 'Leader? The dictionary says it is: 'A person who leads.'

From this it becomes clear that, even by definition, the Owner/Leader is in a very different position when compared to the levels below. There is now no longer any suggestion you have a physical involvement with your money-making activities. You must accept your money is separate from your company's money.

Finally, unlike Employees, the Self-Employed and Managers, Owner/Leaders don't MAKE money or EARN money, they RECEIVE profits. Notice carefully: Both the words MAKE and EARN imply some measure of physical activity or work. There's no such implication with the word RECEIVE.

Get it?

## Reasons to be an Owner/Leader

To put it simply, the most compelling reason to be an Owner/Leader is the passive income stream it provides. But to get it, you must learn to trust all over again. You must learn to let go. My views on this are simple. If a person isn't good enough to do a particular job, you shouldn't have employed them in the first place. You've all heard the saying a company's best asset is its people. What's the point of having this great asset if you won't use them to their full potential; if you won't trust them with a level of responsibility that allows them to do what they've been hired to do? Would they derive any sort of job satisfaction if they weren't trusted to do their jobs? Of course not. This, by the way, would then begin to impact on the morale of the team, which in turn would affect productivity and finally, profit and your passive income stream.

Another attractive reason for taking the step up the ladder and becoming an Owner/Leader is the new lifestyle you'll have. This is where the fun starts. You see, without the daily pressures of managing the business, you'll be able to relax more, concentrate on your health and spend quality time with your family. .

You'll have the time to start learning all over again. You'll be able to read educational, motivational and business books and attend seminars, lectures and workshops. But most importantly, you'll discover there is a bigger game to be played. You'll probably become involved in some business organizations, and through them, your networking will take off. You'll be exposed to concepts, deals and opportunities you never would have as a Level 2 - Manager, and you will start operating more at the strategic level. You will, probably for the first time, learn to invest –REALLY invest.

## Handling Semi-Retirement

Handling semi-retirement presents a whole set of new challenges, especially to the busy business owner. There are many psychological factors to take into account and there are many pitfalls to avoid. You see, because until now everything had rested on your shoulders, everything had depended on you; this is now no longer the case.

It's funny how most people spend their entire working lives dreaming of the day when they WOULDN'T have to go to work to get paid, yet when the time comes, most find this extremely difficult to deal with it. The feelings of inadequacy, of no longer being of use, or of no longer being in control are very difficult to deal with, unless you change your formula for success.

You can spend time developing your social life now you no longer have to trade time for money. You can spend time finding new friends and joining a whole new social circle. You will slowly but surely find, as you work at it, it will become easier to let go of the business, particularly from an operational point of view. If you can't, you might just be sabotaging all you've achieved in business so far.

As your level of financial security improves – and it should have dramatically by now – you'll find you actually stop spending. I know this may sound strange, but believe me, you'll find there just isn't anything more you need to buy. You see, by now you will have enough toys: cars, computers, cameras, television sets, hobbies, you name it, you'll have it all by now, and more.

Your lifestyle will have changed beyond your wildest dreams and, after a while, you'll find yourself looking for fresh challenges.

Suddenly you'll discover the motivation to strive further.


**Moving Up from The Owner/Leader**

So what does it take to move up to the next level – to that of the Investor at Level 4?

The first thing you'll need to be doing at Level 3 is building capital. You'll be accumulating capital to invest in other businesses. This is vital if you want to become really RICH.

By now, you'll have begun setting yourself new business and personal goals. You will have seen the potential for duplicating what you have done in your first business and will realize how easy it is to do again. If it worked once for you, do you think it will work again? Of course it will. Why re-invent the wheel? It's much simpler to use the same systems again and again.

Level 4 is all about investing, and if you are to succeed at this level, you will need to learn as much as you can about investing. You see, what you will be aiming at here is to MAKE MONEY WITH MONEY to create WEALTH. Understand you used to make money with time, but now you make it with other people's time and by having your money make money. The name of the game is to find a company that isn't performing anywhere near its true potential, buy it at a rock bottom price, build it up quickly using all the knowledge, skills and systems you have learned or developed, and then to sell it for a premium price.

Finding these opportunities will be a whole new challenge, and will by now be something you will relish. You might come across them through your business or social network; you might find them by just being observant. Others might advertise the fact they are looking for a new owner, while others still might approach you directly.

You also need to find good jockeys – good people with whom to build up these companies. It may be that some who are already working for you can be transferred to your new acquisition. You will know some through other business dealings. You might have to find them through the traditional method of advertising and interviewing.

A sure-fire indicator you're ready for the next move up the ladder is you're getting uncomfortable again. You're itching for a new challenge. You're not the king anymore.

'Why you should move – it's harder?' - you might question. Well, yes and no. You see, the higher up the ladder you climb, the more FUN it gets. Also, you won't be WORKING harder, just PLAYING for bigger stakes. And you'll be well on your way to getting RICHER…

## Level 4 – The Investor

Investors take a very different view to their business and their business goals. Their basic catch phrase is 'Let's grow.' You see, Investors have a very different way of thinking when compared to those on the previous levels. They think according to what I call the RULE OF ZEROS.

This rule can be simply put as: What is your level of zeros? Or how many zeros are you comfortable playing with? What is your day-to-day number of zeros?

Let's look at an example. Take a house that is on the market for $10,000,000. How many potential buyers might there be for the house? Very few, I would suggest. But if you had a house that was selling for $100,000, how many buyers would there be in the market now? Lots.

When you think about it, amounts with just one zero are like pocket money. $10 or even $20, it doesn't really make much difference. When we start dealing with two zeros, we're probably talking about your first job, aren't we? $300 a week or even $900 a week is really nothing more than the salary we would expect an employee to earn.

To move up the scale to the three zero range, you've either got to be in sales, management or a profession.

To add another zero, you really need to be in business. This is where I ask a very simple question: "How many zeros do you sell in your business every day?" If you're selling a $2 item, that is an item that has no zeros, you really need to sell a massive amount to make a million dollars, don't you? Yet if you are selling an item that costs a half-million dollars, you only need to sell a few to have a very good month.

Several years ago, if a deal was likely to make me tens of thousands of dollars, I would certainly have put my time and effort into ensuring I had every chance of securing it. Then as I progressed up the scale, I would only focus on deals that would make me hundreds of thousands of dollars. But now, if a deal's not making me millions of dollars, it's not worth my time, as time is my most valuable asset.

You see, as you move up the ladder, basically what's happening is the number of zeros are changing. That's why when people get into property, they get rich much faster as they are playing with probably five zeros or more. Just think; a 10% shift in a six zero number is still five zeros!

Let's consider another example. If you are earning a two zero income, what sort of change do you have to make in your life if you want to dramatically increase your lifestyle? A HUGE change. Understand this: if you want to change your financial situation, you have to change your financial situation. You can't expect a small change to bring big results.

As an Investor, you basically make your money selling businesses, not running them. To put it in a nutshell, you achieve this by buying businesses, building them up and then selling them to other people.

## The Entrepreneurial Mindset of the Investor

Because Level 4 is all about INVESTING, or MAKING MONEY WITH MONEY to create WEALTH, you'll be sufficiently removed from the day-to-day running of your business to concentrate on the task at hand.

Operating at this level, you'll want to keep things SIMPLE. Forget about setting up complicated business structures and reporting relationships. Avoid the temptation of empire building. Your immediate goal is the creation of wealth through buying and selling businesses. That's all. You can, of course, aim to buy and sell many businesses each year. Buy one at a rock bottom price, build it up, and then sell at a premium price. Use the proceeds from the sale, or some of them at least, to buy investment property and stocks. Read my book Real Money, Real Estate to find out more about winning the Real Estate game by establishing Property Wealth Wheels. Do this time and time again, using the knowledge and systems you've learnt before.

This brings me to another important concept; LEVERAGE. You'll be looking to exert as much leverage as you can in your business dealings at this level. If you are going to be building up businesses, chances are you will be making use of the same or very similar THINGS or SERVICES you will be buying from various suppliers. This is where you will be making use of bulk buying or the loyalty factor to get the best possible prices. You see, what you're ultimately aiming to achieve here is to acquire businesses as cheaply as possible, then to build them up into a saleable commodity that has real intrinsic value, through leverage, so other business owners will want to buy them.

Understand this: most people looking to buy a business want one that has already been built up by someone else. They want a going concern. They want one that has been set up properly and is making a demonstrable profit. They want to be able to see all the systems are in place and everything is running smoothly, just as much as they will want to examine the books and financial data.

It may seem obvious, but one of your basic goals when buying these businesses is to get a GOOD DEAL. It doesn't matter in the least whether you happen to like the business you're looking at, or whether it is making a good profit. The deal must be very attractive. It must make good business sense.

And never pay the full asking price – always aim to buy wholesale. If you think about it, why would you contribute towards someone else's profit if you are buying a struggling business – one that isn't doing well at all and about to go under? If it were thriving with good systems in place, then you wouldn't be looking at it in the first place, would you? There'd be little room for improvement and little chance of achieving a dramatically higher price for it when the time came for selling. And, it wouldn't be contributing towards achieving your business goals and creating wealth.

By now, you'll be having a tremendous amount of fun, buying and selling businesses and building up your own personal wealth. Things will be starting to happen at different paces, different intensities and different levels. Unless you're careful, you could find yourself drawn back into the thick of things. You could become bogged down and unable to continue finding, buying and selling businesses. You'll realize what you need is a PRESIDENT.

## The Investor's Relationship with Money

At Level 4, you need to learn how to invest the money you make from your passive income stream. The Investor's word for money is RETURN ON INVESTMENT. The Investor thinks only about return on investment. It's all about CAPITAL, and what level of return they can get for investing it.

I said earlier business is just a game. If you accept this analogy, then think of your return on investment as the winnings.

The return on investment a Investor makes comes down to one thing: they understand they no longer trade time for money. Instead, what they're doing is looking for the best investment return.

In reality, the problem faced by most people is they are so busy making enough money to simply exist they don't have enough time to find the good deals. This is because it has been so ingrained into their thinking they must be SPECIALISTS they miss all the opportunities that come their way. They still have the tendencies to get down to doing the work, rather than taking their capital and placing it in places where they can get the best returns.

At Level 4, you no longer need to put in the time and effort to achieve your goals, you only need to use your knowledge and money. You need to leverage them to your best advantage. Understand this; many people are quite happy with a 10% or 15% return on investment. They are because they don't know any better; they don't have much knowledge. But if you want to be rich, you need to acquire as much knowledge as you can, and then you need to apply that knowledge, together with your own money and the principle of Leverage, so it can begin working for you. You also need to ensure you get a Return OF Investment first, then a Return ON Investment.

This is a good time to consider the definition of an investor. According to the dictionary, the noun investor is: 'a person who invests money.' Now, going one step further, the definition of Return on Investment is stated as: 'give as a profit.' There is no work or action implied. The key here is not WORK, but PROFIT. Get it?

But let's not forget all about the work. Just because it's not the Investor who is doing the work, someone's got to do it. As the old saying goes, there's nothing for nothing..

So who's doing the work then? Well, for starters, it's not you. The 'work' you're doing can rather be thought of as strategizing. You are doing all the planning and directing; all the THINKING type of work. It's your TEAM that does the WORK. This is why it's so important to concentrate on TEAM BUILDING earlier on as a Level 2 Manager. And this is why it's so important to choose a good Managing Director and President. Getting this right will free you up so you can get on with the job of buying and selling businesses. It will also allow you the time to pick the right strategies to meet your own personal goals and needs.

**Reasons to be a Investor**

The whole aim of the game at this level is to buy back your time so you can really start playing the game of creating real wealth. You'll be operating in a very different world here, and to do so successfully, you'll need to change a few things. For starters, you'll probably have to change the way you think. That's right – the way you think determines your reality. You've first got to think big before you can achieve big results. Forget about aiming for a 15% return on investment, aim for 200% instead. Think of yourself as the very best in business. Tell yourself each and every day that you ARE rich, and then you will begin to behave like a rich person does. Tell yourself you are a money magnet, and then you'll come across many interesting propositions you wouldn't have noticed before. You see, your mind will become far more aware of the opportunities that cross your path, and it will recognize them.

It's at the level of Investor you'll be solidifying your passive income into real wealth. But to do this, you first have to learn as much about business investing as you can. You need to learn as you go, by trial and error. Now it doesn't only have to be your trials and errors, it can be those made by other people before you. That's right; learn from other people's mistakes. This is the only way you can learn.

In order to grow, the Investor has to first learn, and master, the following, in this order:

- **Business.** Read, understand and apply what you have learnt by reading this book. You must learn how to invest in businesses; how to buy whole companies. Understand this; there is nothing that will give you a better return than buying a whole company, fixing it then selling it. What determines the value of a property? Revenues and profit. And you pay no tax on the massive capital gain you can make when you sell. Business ranks first because it has very low liquidity. They are very easy to invest in.

- **Real Estate.** Read my book Real Money, Real Estate. It contains the most amazingly powerful, yet simple, secrets to winning the Real Estate game. Property ranks second because it's slow – they go up and down in value slowly.

- **Stock Market.** To succeed here, you really need to become a sophisticated investor first. You see, the government has regulations governing this – it's called the Sophisticated Investor Regulation. You need to have over $1,000,000 and an annual income of at least $250,000 before you're allowed to participate in high-level investments. And it's here that you can make the most money. Read as much as you can (there are many very good books available on the subject) and attend as many courses as possible. But remember, it is most important you become a millionaire first. The stock market is ranked third because it is the most complex of the three.

The central theme for successfully operating at this level is to buy businesses wholesale, then channel the profits from them when you sell into Real Estate and stocks that will continue to grow. It's a sad fact that the major reason most people fail at this level is because they've made one mistake too many and don't want to make any more. They give up and revert to Level 3 before they taste success. Remember, it's OK to make mistakes.

Apart from all the fun you'll have operating at this level, there are other sound business reasons for doing so as well.

The first is to BUILD A REPUTATION. This is very important, as you will need to have good, reliable networks to act as intelligence-gathering tools. It's a fact all the best deals are done by people who are well connected. So often those in the know get to hear about a business going on the market long before it is ever advertised in the classified advertisements in the local newspaper. Business brokers call me all the time as soon as they list a business for sale, and by the time it is advertised, I have examined it thoroughly and discarded it for whatever reason. And you can be sure I'm not the only one they call – everyone else with a good reputation as a buyer of businesses will also be on every broker's telephone list.

Another good reason for becoming a Investor is, of course, to BUILD WEALTH. It is also the way to build wealth quickly.

To BUILD A TEAM is another compelling reason for operating at this level. I can't stress enough how important this is.

At the Investor level, you'll certainly LEARN a lot. You'll learn about how to MAKE MONEY WITH MONEY, you'll learn about CORPORATE STRUCTURE, you'll learn about TAXATION, and you'll learn about being a DIRECTOR.

## Buy, Build and Sell

On your journey to riches and true wealth, your STOCK IN TRADE from here on in is all about buying, building and then selling businesses. That's right, that's what you'll be doing. I'll let you in on the specifics later on in the book, and I'll show you everything you need to know about it. But at this point, just remember this is your primary focus.

Buy, Build and Sell will become your motto as a Level 4 Investor. You'll be using your passive income to buy an undervalued business at rock bottom price, then either fixing it for a quick sale or finishing it for a very much more profitable sale a little later on. Remember the value of a business is only determined by two things; revenues and profit. Buying one that's producing very little profit isn't worth very much, yet selling one that produced a very healthy profit will fetch a high price.

The three ways you get a business are to start it yourself, to buy it retail or to buy it wholesale.

The next stage involves either fixing or finishing a business. What you'll be aiming at doing here is building it up so it produces a healthy profit that will, in turn, allow you to ask a very much higher price for it than what you bought it for. This, incidentally, is the area that frightens most people. Yet, as you'll soon discover, there are only five things you need to do to grow a business. That's right – only five.

Finally, when it comes to selling the business, there are a number of strategies you could consider, like providing vendor finance, management buyouts, finding an employee with a payout, selling the business one part at a time or franchising it. These options will be discussed in more detail later on in the book.

Buying a business that represents a good deal, building it into a viable, profitable concern with the aid of a good team and a good jockey, and selling it at a premium price so you achieve the maximum profit, is what your major task will be.

Yet as you become good at it, you will be amazed at how rapidly the profits mount and your personal wealth grows. But there will come a time when you ask yourself whether you should consider a move up the ladder to the final level. After all, you had always fancied yourself as something of an entrepreneur, even though you hadn't fully appreciated the real meaning of the term at the time. And furthermore, you have begun to see the real potential that awaits you out there in the business world.

You might even begin thinking that, since all the really hard work now lies well behind you, surely moving up to Level 5 is nothing more than changing gear and putting your foot down a bit harder?

## Buy, Renovate, Sell

Sometimes your intention might not be to build a business you have acquired. You might just want to renovate it so you can realize the quick profit that might be required to finance a more important business objective.

Deals like this don't warrant spending too much on them. You could have, for instance, bought a business for zero down. With a little bit of work, you could have the business performing very much better. It would then be sellable and whatever you sell it for would be a profit. A client of mine bought a coffee shop for $5,000 from a person who had paid $132,000 for it two years previously. It was just making ends meet. When he took a good look at the business, he found there were only 21 coffee cups. So all he did to double the businesses profit was to buy another 21 coffee cups. It was that simple.

Deals in this category are quick deals. Treat them as part of your stock in trade.

## Moving Up from Investor

OK, so you've made the decision to give it a go and move up to the last rung of the ladder, to see if you have what it takes to operate as a true Entrepreneur. What then are the important concepts you must come to grips with?

Firstly, you will need to get a very good understanding of CORPORATE STRUCTURE. You will need to know how to set up a structure that can accommodate various businesses in such a way everything works to your advantage. For instance, you may want to consider establishing a holding company to hold the shares of subsidiary companies. Needless to say, there are tax ramifications to the way you set up your corporate structure, and this needs to be considered vary carefully.

You will be on a steep learning curve now, and as I've said before, don't be frightened by this. If you stop learning, you'll shrivel. Remember the story of the tree? I've found TO LEARN YOU MUST TEACH.

Teaching is certainly one of the best methods of learning as it forces you to really think about what it is you're trying to teach. You will need to consider what exactly it is you're trying to get across, how you can do it, and whether there are easier ways. This is a marvellous way to re-examine your beliefs and understanding of business systems, methodologies and concepts, and could lead to new ways of doing things.

Teaching is also not only one of the best ways of ensuring the long-term survival of your team; it's also a great team-building exercise.

To GROW, you must SELL. Do enough deals to be considered a Master. People will then want to invest with you. You will then find yourself dealing with other people's money, which will begin leading you to the last level, that of the Entrepreneur.

'To grow you must sell' is a fundamental rule you will be observing by now. And you will have discovered as you grow, so too will you start behaving more and more like an Entrepreneur. You will find yourself moving towards the next level.

You will also have seen the benefits of BUYING WHOLESALE and SELLING RETAIL. This will by now be second nature, and EVERYTHING WILL BE COMING TOGETHER. You will be itching for more …

So why move up? Why indeed, especially seeing you will most probably be enjoying a fabulous lifestyle. You will have everything you've ever wanted, and you'll be very comfortable operating at this level.

Except …

## Level 5 – The Entrepreneur

This last level is the one that, to me, is the most exciting. This is the one where the true capitalist operates. You see, it's at this level where you make money by RAISING CAPITAL. You are using other people's money to build paper assets like stocks, shares, franchises, licenses, and royalties.

Think of it this way; true entrepreneurs use other people's money to make money. Understand this: the reason I run seminars all over the world and write books on how to succeed in business is to build my reputation, so when I take companies public, I have a whole lot of investors ready and waiting to jump in and participate. This is part of my business strategy; it's what I do.

Consider this: What is it Bill Gates, the world's richest man, sells? Does he sell computer software, information, solutions, or systems? What Bill Gates sells is shares in Microsoft. What he sells to create his own personal wealth is shares in Microsoft.

You see, although Microsoft makes good profit, it doesn't make anywhere near enough to make him the world's richest person without him selling part of his company. True entrepreneurs build businesses they can take public. This allows them to gain immediately, or overnight, a massive amount of wealth.

This is where, I believe, most people can go if they know how. But they do, of course, need to have the desire to get there. Many people I come into contact with say, "But Brad, all I want is to get to Level 3." Guess what? As soon as they get there, they want to get to Level 4. As soon as they get to any level, they always want to look at the next, to see what it's like.

But back to Level 5. Remember this: The moment you get to the point where the money is coming in and you no longer have to work, when it doesn't matter whether you get out of bed or not on any particular day, THE GAME HAS JUST BEGUN. At this level, it's a totally different way of thinking. Remember the Number of Zeros Rule?

At this level, you'll be SELLING RATHER THAN BUYING. At Level 4 the emphasis was on buying, building and selling. Now the name of the game is selling. Selling at a different level. You'll be selling franchises or shares in your companies rather than the companies themselves in once-off deals. You'll be selling the investments you've created. These will generally be paper assets to you, but to others, they will be major investments. And when you consider the cost of creating them has usually been zero, the huge profits you'll make from selling them is really exciting. The real buzz operating at this level is what you're basically doing is creating something out of nothing. Sounds odd, I know, but think of it this way: you got going when you started off on your own, slaving away for little or no perceivable return. Then you built up the business to the stage where you no longer needed to be doing all the work in order to earn a living. Then as you realized the potential, you started looking around for other businesses to buy, build up and sell.

This bought you a whole new lifestyle. And it became fun. Then, through leverage, the ball got rolling and you implemented a corporate structure. Your business really began to grow and your income stream flowed stronger than ever before. And now, as a true entrepreneur, you've picked up the pace dramatically, only this time it's being done with other people's money! You are now creating wealth out of nothing. You are basically creating business ventures out of nothing.

At this level, you act as a VISIONARY. You will have the time to sit back and take a long, hard look at the big picture. You will also have the business networks in place to assist you, and the reputation to make it all possible. You will be a dreamer - a dreamer with a vision. It has often been said all the best ideas start with a simple dream. How true that is. But it is no good just dreaming – you need to take ACTION to make your dreams come true.

Sell the dream, and then work like heck to make it a reality. Never give up. And stay focused and committed. Always keep your mind focused on what isn't real but soon will be.

And then trust yourself, and your team, to turn it into reality.


## The Entrepreneurial Mindset of a True Entrepreneur

To get to this level, you've got to have learnt along the way. You have to have gathered knowledge. You now need to change the way you think. You see, you can't be rich if you don't think like a rich person does. It's that simple.

Changing the way you think involves the following four-step process:

- **Idealization.** Create your ideal world in your mind. Think big. Include everything you ever dreamed of.

- **Visualization.** Picture that ideal world as if it were real. Do this twice each day, at 10am and again at 10pm, when you have some quiet time. Spend ten minutes each session thinking about your ideal world.

- **Verbalization.** Talk about your ideal world as if it were real.

- **Materialization.** Things will now start to happen, whether you like it or not. Your ideal world will begin to become a reality. Opportunities will present themselves, you will meet influential people and your dreams will begin to come true.

The true entrepreneur makes money by raising capital, or to put it another way, by using other people's money to make money.

If the true entrepreneur has a catch phrase, it would surely be: 'Not with my money, you don't'.

The true entrepreneur is a visionary, dreaming of what could be. The true entrepreneur is able to see clearly that which does not yet exist.

The true entrepreneur already has a passive income stream as well as physical assets. The true entrepreneur already has wealth. But what will be achieved at this level is becoming rich through the addition of paper assets.

One other thing: you've all heard of ... Bulls and Bears. How does this relate to the true entrepreneur? It's all about mindset ... Bulls bet the market is going up and Bears bet it is going down. But there's one other character I'd like to introduce to you, and that's the Pig. Pigs are those people who just have no idea what's going on. They take tips and bets on anything they can, which in reality is nothing more than the leftovers from the real investors. And bear in mind you make money a lot faster as a Bear. This is because the market usually drops really fast and climbs relatively slowly.

## The Entrepreneur's Relationship with Money

Entrepreneurs don't have to work for their money. They certainly don't trade time for money, and they don't rely on profits as their primary source of income. They may be interested in the return on investment some of their dealings are producing, but this is really incidental. They make their money by raising capital. They create money by adding value. They make it out of nothing, so to speak.

If there's one thing the entrepreneur keeps his or her eye on each and every day, it's the share price. This could be considered the Entrepreneurs stock in trade. Their relationship with money is, therefore, through the stock market.

To operate successfully at this level, you don't rely on your own money, and you certainly don't need your own money in order to do very well here. That's the beauty of it – your money is busy working away very nicely for you all on its own, unaffected by your business dealings. Well, that's not quite true – it is affected in that an income stream that flows whether or not you get out of bed in the morning is constantly increasing it.

The Entrepreneurs dream is to OWN NOTHING BUT CONTROL EVERYTHING. Think of it this way: You have chosen the franchise route for your company. You have set up all the systems and procedures to make the business a roaring success. You have then gone to market to sell it, but instead of simply selling it once, you sell it thousands of times over. The amount of effort remains the same, but look at the return. You now have thousands of new owners in your business. You now effectively own nothing, but yet you control it all. The beauty of this is you don't have any of the risks anymore, your franchisees do. It's their business, but you still control it. And you have a fabulous income stream.

So, how does this all fit in with what the term 'entrepreneur' actually means? Is there something in the dictionary that would throw some more light on it? According to the book of words, an entrepreneur is: 'A person who organizes and manages a commercial undertaking.' The over-riding impression is one of loftiness, of working at a strategic level, of seeing the big picture. The key attribute seems to be one of RESPONSIBILITY.

## Reasons to be an Entrepreneur

Although it may seem obvious, there are many good reasons for wanting to be an entrepreneur. For starters, it's a fact the richer you are THE LESS YOU PAY FOR. Now I'm not being flippant here, but it's true. And it doesn't matter which tax jurisdiction you are operating under, every tax system favours those in business. You see, everything you buy is written off as a business expense. EVERYTHING.

Entrepreneurs have INFLUENCE, there's no denying that. And influence brings with it other advantages like information and opportunity (both business and personal).

Entrepreneurs also have the ABILITY TO ACHIEVE. There is great personal satisfaction to be had in being able to achieve something – anything. And believe me, the higher up the ladder you are, and the richer you are, the more you can achieve. At Level 5 you can truly achieve on a grand scale, and the personal satisfaction achieved as a result is so much more of a thrill.

Of course, like anything in life, it's not all a bed of roses. It's at this level that you'll discover the need to give back. I am actively involved in running my own charity, and I also support many other worthy causes in a big way. So do most other successful entrepreneurs. You still need to be astute, to have sharpened skills and that sort of thing. But perhaps most of all, you need to know how to get investors...

## Getting Investors

As I mentioned earlier, my strategy for getting investors revolves around my REPUTATION. I spend a lot of effort building my reputation so I have credibility. Now there are many different strategies you could use to build your reputation, but writing books and holding seminars is the way I go about it.

Another invaluable resource has got to be your TEAM. Right throughout this book I have stressed the importance of building a good team. If prospective investors see you have the best team available working for you, they will be more inclined to invest as it means they will then have the best team working for them, too. Prospective investors do check out more than just the financial data when they are deciding whether or not to invest in a particular company. Ever noticed the best companies seem to have the best people working for them? It's no coincidence, I can tell you. And it's not that they carn better money there, either. Success breeds success.

So, seeing we are on the subject of money, let's take a look at what money is. According to our trusty dictionary, it is: 'coins stamped from metal (gold, copper, alloys), printed noted, given and accepted when buying and selling.' Note the words 'given' and 'accepted'. Interesting that the implication here is some sort of ACTION. Something is happening – there is a giving and a receiving action implicit. If there is an act of giving, but not of receiving, there is no deal. Money is, therefore, the link between the two parties in any transaction.

At Level 5, you will be dealing with the BIG PLAYERS. These are the people with large amounts of money to invest: the serious investors. You will also be targeting the INSTITUTIONS. Institutional money is traditionally invested in the stock market as a major part of their investment strategies. Included here are the insurance companies, the heath funds, the retirement funds, and the property development companies. Major banks, public utilities and other government organizations also have large amounts of money to invest on a regular basis, and they look for attractive investment opportunities both locally and abroad. These institutions don't only stick with the traditional blue chip companies; they also look for new companies that might produce high dividends, albeit at a greater risk.

As you can see, GOING PUBLIC is the greatest single thing you can do to get people to invest in your company. Not only will you be attracting the attention of the institutions, but you'll be appealing to small-time investors as well – punters hoping to get in early and selling as soon as the price begins to move. Opportunistic investors come in all shapes and sizes; many institutions and big-time private investors include an element of risk in their overall investment strategy.

Of course, once you have taken the decision to go public, once you have satisfied all the requirements for a float, and once you have successfully floated the company, you need to keep your investors. Obviously you can't keep them indefinitely holding onto the shares they have bought in a particular company, but you can keep them interested in buying from you every time you float another company. You see, if your floats turn out to be good investments, if they not only provide good dividends to your shareholders but also give them a very nice capital gain when they sell the shares, they will come back for more later. They will be more likely to invest again when you float another company. It's all about having a good reputation, isn't it?

**Playing the Game vs. Retirement**

So, you've made it to Level 5 and you are doing very well, thank you very much. What's next? Is there anywhere to move up to?

This is a very good question, but consider this: you'll probably find by now that it's the game you enjoy. Remember at the outset I said business is nothing more than a game? Most people who are at this level will agree with me, and so will you I'm sure.

Most people at this level also realize they need to start giving something back. They may decide to become involved with one or two of their favourite causes or charities, or they may wish to start one of their own. I personally have a passion for assisting children in trouble. Others become benefactors to scientific research organizations and educational facilities. But whatever you decide, you'll find immense satisfaction in giving something back to the community.

By playing the game, you'll also find you start building absolutely amazing companies, the likes of which you never would have thought possible just a few short years before. When I started out not long ago, I never dreamed that before I turned 30, I would be the International Chairman of a global company. And I'm not alone. There are many success stories all over the world.

Where does it all end, then? When do you retire?

Well, I retired financially when I was 26 years of age. But that didn't mean I just sat around and vegetated. Far from it. I am more active now than ever before, and I am having an immense amount of fun. You see, the word 'retirement' doesn't exist in my vocabulary, and it shouldn't in yours either.

This is retirement. Enjoy it. If you've come this far, you deserve it.

# Part 3

# ▌ Buy, Build and Sell

This is the very basic motto of the Level 4 Investor. This is the level where you start to make some serious money. In fact, if you never progress to Level 5 you can still become extremely wealthy here at Level 4. Not Rich, but Wealthy.

Now, Levels 0,1,2 and 3 are handled in detail in my other books, tapes and video's, but if you want to move through them extremely quickly, you'll need to work with one of my *ACTION International* Business Coaches. They can help you with your Business Plan, putting the systems in place in your business, building a team and most importantly, they will Coach you through putting marketing systems and strategies in place and making more money without having to work IN your business.

Other ways to learn Level's 0 through 3 are simply through trial and error, which of course just takes a lot of time or, through playing my board-game, LEVERAGE. It's the game of business and by playing it you'll learn how to set your business up to work without you. The reason I recommend learning through games is so you're actually doing what you need to do in real life. It also makes it much easier for your brain to put into ACTION all the new concepts you'll be learning when you get to your place of business each and every day.

Level 5, on the other hand, is not something that's written about in any book. Level 4 I teach just once a year at my 5-day Entrepreneurs Training Workshop, but Level 5 is something I only teach to 20 people annually. These people I select personally, because they have succeeded at Level 4.

So, right now the game is Level 4 … how to build amazing wealth to back up the cashflow of your business. Remember one very important fact here though – "NEVER sell your business until you have a business with greater cashflow to replace it".

This is the most important factor in moving from Level 3 to Level 4. Far too many times I've seen people get all excited about getting their first business up and running without them, that they want to sell it and take a big cash payment. After tax, paying any debts and things like that, you won't be left with enough to make a real difference. Leave that business running and go find your next one.

When you take the step up to Level 4, you'll need to start remembering your everyday motto is 'Buy, Build and Sell.' What you're basically doing is buying an undervalued business and paying as little in cash as you can negotiate. You then build the business through team building, marketing, sales, systems and so on, then sell it for several multiples of what you paid for it, all inside 6 to 12 months. In other words, your businesses become your 'Stock in Trade'.

How many can you run at one time? Well, I recommend you start with one, and start as your own jockey, running it day-to-day, building it up as you go, so you learn what to do and what not to do along the way.

Sell that one and move on. Be the jockey again for the second one, and train yourself a new jockey who you will take with you to the next business and so on, all the while collecting passive income from your main business.

The number of businesses you buy ultimately depends upon how many you find, fund and fix.

That brings me to three important concepts. Let's take some time considering them.

FIND ... as many good deals and turn them into great deals using everything you're about to learn.

FUND ... use someone else's money at every turn and only ever use your own money as working capital (if at all).

FIX ... put a jockey in place, get them building for you, working without you, at a profit and then whether you get a quick sale or not it doesn't matter. Your holding costs are actually a profit, so hold onto it if it won't sell.

So, here's how to make this all happen ...

## Three Ways Of Buying A Business

This is where most people get it wrong. In fact, the biggest mistake you can make in business is to buy a business where you know how to do what the business sells. In other words, remember the hairdresser who buys a salon, or the accountant who buys an accounting firm.

Why is this the number one mistake? Because you treat it like a job rather than a business. Remember, you're an entrepreneur not an employee.

In a few pages you'll be able to learn the fundamental rules of what to do when buying a business. Follow these rules and you'll do well. Break them and you'll suffer a great deal of pain with the businesses you buy. So, before you even think of getting into business, follow the rules.

One other point you should note. Buying a business doesn't always mean parting with CASH. I'll run through how to buy a business with No Money Down shortly, but don't get any ideas that just because you're buying a business you need to have hundreds of thousands of dollars in the bank.

Put simply, people will sell things for much less than they're worth if they have enough reasons.

This brings up one extremely important point that is worth remembering. The profit you make is in the purchase, NOT in the sale. In other words, it doesn't matter how much you sell it for, if you bought it very cheaply, you'll still make money.

That's why when you're looking to get into business you can get burnt by one very powerful emotion – impatience. Keep looking until you find something that is perfect, not just something that's almost it, but something that's great.

Walk away from more deals than you take. Far too often people take a deal because it's the only deal they have in front of them. Here's a simple formula you can follow when you're buying businesses.

Look at 50 businesses, make an offer on ten of them, negotiate three of the ten to get a great deal, and then you should be able to get finance for just one of the three. Here's what this really means.

Out of 50 businesses you see, 40 will not meet your rules so you shouldn't make an offer on them. Ten will meet the rules so you will make an offer. Of the ten you make an offer on, you should only enter into any form of negotiation on only three of them. If more than three of the ten get to the negotiating stage, then you're offering too much.

Then your financiers will knock two of the three back. That's right; only one in three business plans you write will get financed. If one banker turns you down, go to another. If 20 possible financiers turn you down, take the hint and go find another business.

**Starting It Yourself**

So often Level 0 Employees assume the best way to get into business is to put in a lot of hard work starting it yourself, then financing the business through cashflow. I know this seems logically the best way to get into business, but hopefully I'll convince you otherwise.

When you buy an ongoing business you're buying a simple memory. A memory in the minds of the people who have driven past, who have seen a sign, who have read an advertisement, or most importantly who have shopped there before. It's not really the reputation as much as it's the recognition factor you're investing in.

So, think of this; what price are you paying for almost everything you need if you start the business yourself? That's right; in most cases you're paying retail. Giving someone else the profit. I know you can go to the wholesaler and the auctions to get started, butwhen you buy everything in one place you get an amazing discount. Not because of logic, but because of emotion.

But here's the real cost. You're paying retail when you're buying customers. Let me explain this. If you spend $1,000 in advertising and get 10 new customers, then you're paying $100 ($1,000/10) per new customer.

In business today, buying customers is the most expensive purchase you'll ever make. Buying a going concern - and we'll talk about how to do this with no money down later on - means you not only get the equipment for much less than you would if you bought them one piece at a time, but you also get the customers thrown in for free.

Ask anyone who started a new company what the hardest part was, and by far and away, all will agree it was getting customers. I know when you buy an already running company they may not have a lot of great customers, but think of it this way …

You are almost at break-even already every week with a business you buy that's running at a small loss. That's got to beat starting with no customers and no cashflow at all.

Starting a business from scratch is once again wasting your most valuable asset – time. Think about it for a moment. Start your own business and it will take you somewhere between one and five years to become profitable. Buy an existing business that's already profitable or just about profitable and you've saved yourself those one to five years.

This is one very important lesson most people wish they had learnt when they first started out. Someone once said to me the biggest reason people fail in business is a lack of start-up capital … yes that's true, but only because they started the business themselves and had to pay retail for everything.

Most of the businesses I buy for little or no money down are the ones that were start-ups about one or two years before, and the person running them had just run out of steam. You don't want to be this person; selling a business you've started to someone who's just read this book. So, onto the second possible way …

## Buying Retail

Obviously when you buy something and pay the retail price for it, you're giving someone else the profit. Suffice to say, there are only a few occasions when I'll recommend anyone do this.

Firstly though, what do I mean by 'Buying Retail' …

Generally when you look in the paper or call a broker they're going to show you the advertised price of a business for sale. To me you're paying retail if you buy the business for a price anywhere near the price they've advertised it for. And by anywhere near I mean anything more than half of what they've advertised it for.

Even with this in mind there are several reasons I'll recommend Level 0, 1, 2 and 3's should use this purchasing method.

However, I strictly want to point out it's my suggestion you only ever pay retail for your first few businesses. Once you've bought, built and got these first few running at a profit without you, you've got enough time and money to move on and do Level 4 deals.

**Reason #1** … At least you've got a start. The business is up and running, and making a profit. This profit making is extremely important if you're paying retail. You want built-in profits that give you a planned return on investment before you even have to build the business.

And, if you're paying full price, you want full profits. Make sure you get the previous owner to work with you for up to a month as part of the purchase price to train you. One important thing about the previous owner, though; they're still blinded by what you can't do, based on their experience. Always be willing to try something new, even though they seem to feel it won't work.

**Reason #2** … You're about to learn a whole lot. Whilst I'd still recommend negotiating on the price, remember the main objective of your first business is to learn and grow, and secondly to make money and profits.

**Reason #3** … The most powerful time I suggest it's extremely wise to pay retail is when you're investing into a proven Franchise. Franchising has removed many of the pitfalls for the business buyer. And whilst many of the franchise systems are great, there are also many that are pitiful. So many people starting franchises have no idea how to train you, support you and help you succeed. Be aware the best franchises are generally the ones you will have to pay a solid price for. However, remember to look for profit, not turnover.

If you need help researching franchises, go to my company's website www.franchisemasters.com.au and check out the franchises we have built and have available.

One last point about buying at a retail price; whilst it's not the best way to buy, it's still a solid way for first-time buyers to invest in an already proven system that can fast track both your profits and your learning experience.

## Buying Wholesale

Of course, this is what I recommend. Never pay more than you have to for anything. Remember, you don't make the profit when you sell; you make it when you buy. Far too often people think about what they can sell the business for, rather than saving thousands up front and adding that to your profits at the end.

So, what is 'Buying Wholesale' when it comes to buying a business?

Essentially what we're looking at is a whole new frame of reference about buying stuff. Most people negotiate based on the advertised price. We will from now on, however, negotiate based on the initial price of ZERO. That's right, most people work their way down from the advertised price, I negotiate from a big fat '0' and have them justify why it's worth anything at all.

Now, you're going to have to search a little longer and a little harder to find these deals, but when you get one, it's so worth the wait. The biggest challenge most people have in the negotiation process is patience. I live by a simple negotiation mantra … "I have more persistence than you have resistance".

You see, I'm willing to wait and wait and wait until a deal works, and if the deal never works, then so be it …

If you want to be a great Level 4 or 5, you've got to be willing to walk away from far more deals than you take. It's relatively simple to say, even easier to read, but when it comes down to it, we all want to win, and some will try so hard to win they'll ultimately lose, and lose big time.

Remember; fall in love with the deal, not the business.

I suppose the simplest way to explain the notion of buying wholesale is for you to always know someone has to take a CASH loss. If the person selling to you is taking a profit, then you're NOT.

Most people seem to think I'm ruthless because of this, and maybe I am a little, but the fact still remains. A $1,000 in my pocket is far better than a $1,000 in the pocket of someone I just bought a business from.

Thus, we can never make the mistake of being overly generous when we're buying a business. You'd negotiate hard and long if you were buying stock for your store, so do the same when you're buying the store.

One question that commonly arises when I start to mention buying a business for little or no money is; "Why would they sell it to me for so little?".

Hopefully, you've already thought of a few answers. Most of the answers are emotional rather than logical: Divorce, Sickness, Tiredness, Pregnancy, Travel, or just plain sick and tired of working too many hours for too little money.

I really don't care what the reason, I just want to know the buyer is more motivated to sell than I am to buy. Of course I empathize with them and discuss the pregnancy, and I'm genuine when I tell them that I don't believe I can pay them money for their business. I can help them out and take over their leases, but nothing more.

If I'm hard and nasty about it all, they won't sell to me, but if I'm nice and genuine, many will do a deal with me.

A very important point to keep in mind is every time you go out to look for a new business, you're merely 'Shaking the Tree'. And every now and then when you shake the tree an apple will fall. Sometimes though, you can shake the tree for months for nothing, and then when the time is right, you shake it and a dozen apples fall.

If you're focused on buying wholesale rather than just BUYING, you'll make a whole bunch of money when the 12 fall and then relax for a few months when nothing is falling.

Again, one final point: Buying wholesale takes discipline, it takes following up and abiding strictly by your investment rules. Anyone can go out and pay full price for a business. It takes an artist, an entrepreneur, to make a deal and have everyone leave the table happy.

## Where To Find The Best Businesses

Before I really get into the details on where to find the best deals, I have to be certain I remind you of one thing …

REMEMBER THE RULES …

It's no good getting excited and buying a business you've fallen in love with when in reality you should walk away from more deals than you take.

Remember too that it's the owners who are selling their businesses. They are doing so for all sorts of reasons, many of which won't be apparent initially. And most are unlikely to tell you the real reasons up front. So unless you assume the worst (from their point of view) and base your options on that, you'll never know just what you might have achieved.

Remember too brokers and agents want a commission. If you're buying through a broker or agent, the asking price, as well as the finally agreed price, will take this into account. You will end up paying for this.

And it's always worth bearing in mind some businesses aren't for sale until you make an offer. Have a go; you might surprise yourself.

### Newspapers

Newspapers are a great way to find businesses for sale – in fact they're my favourite way. Most newspapers have a specialized business section in which there will be classified ads for businesses for sale. I love these ads because they tell you everything you need to know. Let me explain: Around 70% of advertisers in newspapers are business owners; the remainder are brokers. And owners sell on emotion. They want to sell because they want out. They are sick to death of their business and hate going there every day.

Business Brokers often run display advertisements here too, with many of their listings mentioned in the one display advert. It's fairly easy to identify which are being handled by a broker and which by the owner.

You will notice some ads include abbreviations like SAV (stock at value) and WIWO (walk in walk out). Make a point of finding out what the abbreviations in your paper mean.

I strongly recommend you follow up the ads that appeal to you with a phone call first. The main aim here is to get as much information as you can about the business by asking questions.

You will also be building rapport with the seller. Sound interested and let them know you buy businesses all the time. Tell them it's important you collect certain pieces of information before you come out to see the business, as you don't want to waste anybody's time. They'll appreciate it.

Find out about weekly revenues and then multiply to arrive at an annual figure. The reason for this is to minimize the chances of them fudging these figures later. You should also ask about annual profit, what they pay themselves in wages, any costs they remove from the business, fixed outgoings like rent, and an idea of the approximate variable expenses such as wages.

Then ask questions about how they go about marketing the business. You should also ask questions that will enable you to see whether the business complies with my seven rules for buying a business – I'll get to them later in the book. I would suggest, however, you prepare your list of questions first so you don't forget any during your conversation with the seller.

Once you have all this information, you should be in a better position to decide whether it would be useful to visit the business. You will certainly be able to gather more bits of information this way should you need to.

## Magazines

There are various specialist magazines available catering for businesses for sale. These can provide excellent leads, but remember, brokers usually publish them. This means you are more than likely going to be dealing with a broker when you respond to an ad found in these magazines.

Another important point to bear in mind when browsing through magazines to find businesses for sale: Businesses that advertise in magazines are usually selling retail. You see, it's usually very much more expensive to place an ad in a magazine than it is to run a small classified in the local newspaper. Business owners who just want out are unlikely to be able to justify the additional cost. It's usually the seller who's aiming for a premium price, or at least a retail one that can afford to place magazine ads.

Sellers who opt for a magazine ad can also usually afford to wait for the right buyer to come along. They are usually in no hurry to sell. If they were, they wouldn't be advertising in a publication that only comes out once a month. Magazine ads only usually result in a sale months after they appear.

If you're in the market for a bigger business, and keen to secure some form of vendor finance as part of the deal, then you're more than likely going to come across such opportunities through magazine advertisements. And remember too, when it comes time for you to sell your finished business, this is where you'll get your best responses.

## Brokers and Agents

You'll either love them or hate them, but they can be a great source of new businesses for you to consider if you approach them correctly. What I mean by this is you must build relationships with them. You need to get them working for you. If they know you're in the market for businesses, they will keep you in mind whenever they list a new business for sale. And when they become more familiar with you and your requirements, you'll find they'll call you even before their ads begin running. You'll begin to be offered first bite at the cherry, so to speak.

Developing a good working relationship with Brokers and Agents can really pay off. Don't make the mistake of discarding this as a means to an end.

But remember, they earn their money through charging commissions. One worthwhile benefit of having a good working relationship with a broker is you might be able to negotiate a better commission structure, if you as a buyer are liable to pay one. Most sales transactions require the seller to pay the commission, but in reality, this is done with the money paid by the buyer.

It's also worth considering placing a standing order with a broker. That way you have someone else doing the searching for you. They will regard you as a Premium Client and one worth supporting. You will also be making their job that much easier.

## Shopping Centre Managers and Leasing Agents

For shopping centre managers and leasing agents to work for you, you need to build a good relationship with them. This is how it works ... In most retail shopping centres, one of the clauses in their retail leases says if a tenant falls behind on their rent payments, the centre can repossess the tenant's business to basically make up for the rent. It doesn't happen often, but it does happen.

Take this case as an example. A bookstore had fallen four months in arrears on its rent payments. I asked the Centre Manager what the shop's stock was valued at.

"$180,000," came the reply.

"How much rent is owed?" I asked.

"$25,000," the Manager replied.

"OK, let's negotiate," I responded. "I'll offer you $15,000 for the shop."

"No, I want $25,000," the Manager said.

"OK, I'll give you $25,000."

Did I get a good deal? Of course I did. I had just bought $180,000 worth of stock for $25,000.

I love retail businesses. Most retail business owners are bad rent payers and they have binding contracts. If they can't meet their contractual obligations, they have a problem. What I am doing in offering to buy their business is helping them out. How many of them would like to have three or four years rent hanging over their head after they've closed the business.

Of course, once you have developed a good working relationship with the Centre Manager or leasing agent, you might consider placing a standing order. "Let me know of any businesses that fall behind in their rent payments," you might say. This way you'll also be helping out the Manager and Agent as well.

## Landlords

Landlords have even more vested interest in a business than the Centre Manager or Leasing Agent as they require a business to do well so they can continue to receive rent. When a business can't pay the rent, Landlord's start looking for tenants who can.

If you're close to the Landlord, you could receive first-hand information regarding businesses that might be ripe for an approach. I always keep an eye out for ones that are about to have their premises repossessed by the Landlord. You see, if you take over a struggling business and set about turning it around, the Landlord will love you as you'll be taking steps to ensure the rent continues to be paid.

Landlords usually advertise the fact that they're looking for a new tenant well before the existing one vacates or when it's too late for them and they're stuck with an empty, unproductive space. If you come along with a proposal to take over the lease, he'll love you. You could offer to sign a long-term lease, but remember to negotiate hard. Ask for a rent-free period to allow you to settle down and begin trading.


## Bankers and Receivers

In order to make use of Bankers and Receivers as a source of finding good business deals, I suggest you get yourself known around town. Give out your business card on every occasion. Watch for their ads in the newspapers.

Bankers and Receivers step in when a business fails. Get to know the repossession officials in your local area and stay in contact with them. Talk to them on a regular basis and let them know what interests you. They can be a very lucrative source, as they just have to get rid of businesses for a certain price. Remember, they just want their fee or their loan repaid, and they may be prepared to sell a business for well under what it is really worth.

## Internet

The internet is becoming a more and more important tool all the time. However, it is usually only brokers that use it to any extent at present. I suggest you treat it in the same manner as you would a magazine. After all, it is really nothing more than an electronic magazine.

# Part 4

# How To Raise The Money For Your New Business

When the time comes for you to buy your first business, you'll probably wonder where the money's going to come from. I'll show you in a moment. But first, let me say you might not need any at all. And I don't mean what you think – that you've got loads of cash in the bank and therefore won't need to raise money.

There are two forms of capital – cash and time. If you don't have enough cash capital, you might be able to invest time capital. Both are vital in business, but let's concentrate on money. Remember, the definition of money is coins or printed notes given and accepted when buying and selling.

Now I know most people starting out in business don't have the sort of money they think they will need, but I think you'll be surprised at both how little you'll need and how simple it is to get funding. There are many ways to raise money, as you'll see shortly. Just remember, if one person says no to financing your business idea, go on and try another. If 20 say no, move on and try another idea.

Now; where to find the money. There are seven ways I'll show you.

**Your Own Savings**

OK, so you've had a job and saved up some capital and you want to buy a business. You've scrimped and saved for years, and you've built it up slowly for this very purpose. You want to keep things simple and easy, and prefer not to worry about loans and contracts. The money's there now anyway, and investing it is no real pain, you argue.

That's fine, but there's one problem with this approach. You've already paid tax on the money.

Another problem I have with this approach is I've found people are really too stingy when it comes to spending their own money on what a business needs. They tend to keep their money in reserve, just in case. That's why I recommend you get investment to buy the business but use your own cash as working capital.

## Family and Friends

If you have to borrow money off family and friends, there are three words I want you to remember; 'NOT FOR LONG.'

Family and friends have to be the worst place, emotionally, you could go to raise money because they will all want a say in the running of your business. They will all want to tell you what to do. Believe me when I say family and friends are the worst ever 'SILENT' partners. You will very soon find yourself the subject of what I call Emotional Blackmail. My recommendation – don't do it.

## Bankers

Bankers are the greatest business partners when you can get them. I love the Banks for a couple of very good reasons.

Firstly, unlike family and friends, they usually keep their mouths shut. They don't interfere with the running of your business. They leave that entirely up to you.

Secondly, if you increase the profit of your business ten fold, the bank still wants you to repay the amount you borrowed, plus a little in interest. They are not your equity partners – all they are doing is loaning you some cash. They don't want ten times their money back.

Let me give you some advice about approaching banks for loans. Remember, the best time to approach a bank is at the beginning of the month. You see, the banks have a formula governing how much they can approve each month. So if you come along towards the end of the month and their quota is already allocated, you'll miss out.

Also, don't just go to one bank; approach many. They want security, and will be looking to see what the chances are they will lose their money. How will you repay your loan? What happens if you can't repay it? How will they recover their money? These are the sorts of questions they will be asking.

Take along a Big Fat Business Plan, as it shows them you have done your homework and you are prepared. But be sure to develop your business plan in a way that it becomes a living document, not just something to satisfy the Bank Manager. By making it a pro-active document that identifies all the important goals and stepping stones as well as how they'll be transformed into reality, it will certainly impress your Bank Manager. Remember, a Business Plan must be a step-by-step guide on the future of your business. It must provide you with a road map of how to get from where you are now to where you want to be. It must outline the strategies that will ensure higher revenues and profit margins. If you require help, ask an **ACTION** Coach about the SuccessModel™ Planning System.

If you have a Board of Directors, be sure to include well-known business personalities on it. Invite impressive people to sit on the Board. This will not only indicate to the Bank you have an impressive amount of business knowledge upon which to draw, it will also give you more credibility as a business person.

The Bank may ask for a personal guarantee as a condition of granting you a loan. Your initial reaction to this may be to resist, to try and find another form of security or even try another Bank. The reality of the situation is you will most probably have no option but to give a personal guarantee. And there's absolutely nothing wrong with this. In fact, if it's to finance your first business venture, you'll most probably have no other option but to, so don't let this stop you from getting into business.

## Investors

Investors are an important source of funding when it comes to establishing or buying a business. What I like about them is they usually just want to put money in; they will usually let you get on with running the business and giving them a return of their investment.

Investors take a professional approach to their business dealings. They are not interested in your idea or business as such, and this is what most people fail to realize. You see, what they are looking at is the person that will be running the business. Understand this: Investors invest in the people, not the idea or the business. When you approach an investor, remember it's not the business idea you are trying to sell to them. They are interested in the jockey, not the horse.

Don't forget to ask for other forms of capital if that's what you need. Investors don't only invest money. They may be interested in giving you a loan, or capital, or half and half if that's what you require.

And finally, my suggestion is you offer them equity for their investment but make them the first to receive all or part of their money back before you take any profits.

## Venture Capitalists

Venture capitalists are like farmers; they invest in an idea and make that idea work. They get involved as they have a vested interest. Be very aware they will want to control it all. They will leave you with just a little – say 5 or 20 %. A venture capitalist is more of a senior partner than an investor.

Securing a venture capitalist is an attractive proposition for getting really big businesses up and running. They're also one of the best options available for funding business ideas that hinge on the commercialization of inventions. Venture capitalists are great because they bring the business substantial capital as well as significant hands-on management skills that will most probably be invaluable in getting large business projects up and running.

## Going Public

Going public is only for BIG idea companies. Going public allows you to raise millions, or even billions, of dollars quickly. It's a very specialized area and not too many people will consider this as a serious option. You see, it can cost you anything from a minimum of $150,000 into the millions of dollars to accomplish. However, it remains a great option when you reach Level 5. But remember, the payoff has to be BIG, and only about one in 12 succeed.

## Franchising

The franchise market is a dynamic industry that allows any type of business to grow by distributing products or services. When you expand by selling your trademark and business systems to another person, you adopt the franchise structure. By granting permission as a manufacturer to a distributor or retailer to sell your products, you create the contract of a franchise.

Franchising is an exciting option that allows you to sell your business, over and over again without loosing control of the business. It is an option you could consider if you want to raise a large amount of money quickly.

If you need to ascertain whether your company is franchisable, or if you want to find out more about what is involved in franchising, visit my website www.franchisemasters.com.au

## No Money Down

This is one of the most useful, and least understood, methods of raising money to buy a business. It's so important I'm going to focus on it in some detail.

In the next section, I'm going to teach you four different types of No Money Down deals. I've used them all very successfully myself.

# No Money Down Deals

When I was just 22, I thought I knew it all. Then something happened that proved I didn't. I was having a great time, but ended up loosing a lot of money. I found myself very much in debt.

Not knowing what to do next, I turned to my parents.

My Dad said, "It can't be that bad. Make a list and go and fix it."

I took his advice and did just that.

It took me six months to make back everything I'd lost so I could repay all my debts. How did I do this? I did No Money Down deals based on the one thing I hadn't lost – my knowledge.

I approached many companies saying: "If I can meet these targets, will you give me a percentage of the company?" Most said no, but some said yes. This is how I bought into a few medium sized companies without any money.

I then got stuck in, met all my targets and sold my shares in the businesses, allowing me to repay all my debts and get started all over again.

Now I'm not suggesting it's easy to find deals like this. You need to search high and low. But remember, they do exist.

So, let's take a closer look at the four types of No Money Down Deals I've done …

### Zero Price

I was looking through the newspaper recently and noticed two similar businesses for sale. One had a turnover of $750,000 and an asking price of $350,000. The other had a turnover of $700,000 and an asking price of $120,000. How did these two business owners arrive at their selling prices? They do what most sellers do – they take a guess.

The trouble is if you're a typical buyer, you'll start negotiating around the asking price, not its true value.

I say this is crazy, and always begin by saying: "I'll offer you zero for the business, but I'll take over the leases."

So many times a retail business will be struggling to make ends meet, but can't simply close down because they have leases they have to comply with. In many cases, by offering to take over the leases you will be doing the seller a favour.

I love these types of deals – there's nothing better. The seller can walk away, cutting their losses without having to worry about paying rent till the end of the lease, even though they are no longer renting the premises. The cost of the deal, to me, is simply the cost of the lease.

And remember, in addition to leases covering the rental of the premises, there are also equipment leases you can take over.

So, once you have bought the business, you next need to go to see the landlord. The reason for this is to try and secure a rent-free period.

In a deal I once did, I met with the landlord and said: "I've just started out in business and need to conserve my cash as much as possible. These are my marketing and sales plans that will ensure the business picks up and begins to thrive over the long-term. What I need is a six-month rent-free period. You can build this into the end of the lease, if you like."

He agreed to a three month rent-free period, and I went away confident of turning the business around. You see, my aim was to generate maximum profit during the early stages, as it was during this period I would need to inject some capital into the business.

The landlord was happy because he could see that I was doing everything possible to ensure he would be receiving rent from the business over the long-term. And in any event, my plan was to build the business up and to sell it before the rent-free period had expired. I was looking for a quick turn around.

Another thing I should mention at this stage - when making your offer on a business, always include some clauses like subject to your partner's approval (whether you have a business partner or not), and subject to you finding a suitable manager or staff. But more about this later.

I'd also recommend you run your first few businesses yourself as it will give you experience. And while you'll eventually end up employing people to run the businesses for you, this way you'll know if they are doing a good job or not. You'll also be able to help them improve their performances.

I believe if you start off in a small business and make mistakes, the mistakes will generally be of a small nature. The higher up the ladder you go, the bigger the mistakes tend to get. You see, you make your mistakes at the level of your experience.

There are three keys to succeeding in deals of this type. Firstly, get the vendor to like you. Build rapport by saying how much you like the business. Look for other areas that you have in common with them and show an interest in what they do. This will give you the right to proceed with the two remaining factors that are crucial to securing Zero Price deals.

Secondly, explain to the vendor why the business is not worth anything logically. You could, for instance, highlight the fact it isn't producing much in the way of profit and as a result it's really only producing an average wage. What it amounts to, you might add, is nothing more than a job. You might add that it's not a job your after – you want to buy a profitable business.

You will now be in a position to concentrate on the third key to Zero

Price deals.  Mention you really don't mean to offend them, but your offer will be realistic under the circumstances (you might want to have your accountant or advisor with you to agree with you as you talk your way through your proposal). Offer zero for the business, but say you will take over their leases.


**Vendor Finance**

Have you ever considered asking the seller to finance your purchase? This is my favourite option. It works like this: Suppose you are considering buying a business for $50,000, you ask the vendor to loan you the $50,000.

Let me give you an example. I bought a restaurant from a lady once who owned two restaurants – one in Brisbane and one in Sydney. At the time, the Sydney restaurant was doing very well, but the Brisbane one was struggling. She found herself spending more and more time in Brisbane trying to save it from going under. The result was that her Sydney restaurant started to suffer as well. She took the decision to sell up in Brisbane to allow her to put all her effort into her Sydney business.

She put the restaurant on the market for $74,000. It eventually fell to an advertised price of $34,000. I offered her zero for the business but said I would be happy to take over the lease. She countered, and after negotiating we settled on a price of $12,000. I then said to her that I had a problem coming up with the cash as I needed the dollars to rebuild the business and asked if she would consider a vendor finance deal. Would she lend me the $12,000, I asked?

She said she would accept a payment of $1,000 a month for the next 12 months. Now was that a good deal, or what? Of course it was.

Anyway, I began building up the business real fast, offering a free bottle of wine to anyone who dined there. Of course, I had already made contact with a winery, offering them great exposure in exchange for cheap wine.

Then I put the restaurant back on the market for $35,000. Whenever prospective buyers came around, guess what? The restaurant was always full, and this impressed them enormously. It sold in no time at all.

What's more, I didn't repay the $12,000 I owed immediately. I did it at the rate of $1,000 a month for the next 12 months. I couldn't have got cheaper finance than that.

Vendor's will only consider a finance package if they perceive your price to be fair. These deals can very often be the only ones they will get. This is particularly the case with higher-priced businesses or owners selling due to ill health or to retire. In many of these cases, they want to quit, but have a viable business that carries a big price tag. There aren't many buyers out there that can afford to buy businesses of this size, and often the traditional lenders are more cautious about lending on them.

One benefit here for you as a buyer is you can avoid paying any interest on the loan. Usually it's a straightforward function of the final price over time. But there can be instances when money is only part of the deal. You could make an offer, for instance, that comprises 50% vendor finance and 50% finance from your savings or from a bank.

Be imaginative here when making your pitch.

## Knowledge Buy-In

To successfully use this method, it certainly helps if you have a good reputation – especially if you are a Business Coach, have succeeded in other local businesses or something similar. As I mentioned earlier, this is the method I used to get up and running again, and it worked very well.

What you basically say when making an offer to work with a business is: "If I can reach these goals for your business, will you give me a percentage of the business?" You could, for instance, ask for 30% of the business if you can double turnover within six months.

Many business owners will say no, but some will agree. I have bought into some very solid and large companies this way. But remember, don't do it just because they agree. You need to be sure in your own mind what you are proposing is achievable otherwise you're wasting your time. You also need the rules up front and in writing. You will be investing a lot of your time and knowledge into this business, and you want to be sure you will receive part of the business in return. I suggest using share options here.

The problem with this method is most people simply don't have the knowledge. I can build any business any time because I know how. Once you have this knowledge, it never leaves you. The acquisition of knowledge is the greatest investment you can make. Between the ages of 17 and 21 I attended every seminar that I could, I read over 700 books, I listened to every business tape I could find and watched so many videos I've lost count. And I've found as an investment, the knowledge will pay me back forever.

One final thing; remember partnerships don't work. There can only be one boss, one captain of the ship. Sure, there are many successful partnerships, but they all have clearly defined rules and boundaries.

You'll find only one of them is in charge. Silent partners are OK, but you need to be clear on the rules.

## Landlords

Landlords are another great source of money for buying businesses. You see, they basically give leasing finance.

Let me give you another example. A restaurant owner (yes, another one, not the one from Sydney) couldn't meet his rent payments, forcing the landlord to repossess the restaurant. He now had this complete restaurant with all the tables and chairs, the kitchen and everything. However, landlords aren't in business to run things like restaurants, they own property.

So I rang him up and made an offer on the restaurant. I asked for the usual rent-free period, but this time received a rent reduction instead. Once again, I built up the business and sold within a few months.

When dealing with landlords like this, you need to make sure you can sell. Firstly, you need to sell him on the idea, and secondly, you need to be sure you can sell the business later. They may even want to see proof that you will succeed in business.

Now you know you can get the money, let's consider my rules for buying a business ...

# Part 5

# ▌ Seven Rules for Buying a Business

I was once asked for the difference between a speculator and an investor. My initial response was to talk about timing, how a speculator is in it for the short-term and an investor for the long-term.

I was then left on my own to ponder this question a little further. Eventually I realized my answer was incorrect.

The true difference between an investor and a speculator is embodied in a clearly defined set of INVESTING RULES …

Rules are by far and away the most important part of any investor's success. With a good set of rules you'll be able to consistently create a winning investment result.

There are some things to keep in mind though. The best way to follow your own rules is to have what I call a 'Check Up Person'. It's like having a boss you have to report to, a higher authority you have to obey. I do this so I can be sure I'm not getting caught up in the emotion and excitement of doing the deal, but rather that I'm doing a good deal.

What I'm about to share with you are my absolute MUST OBEY rules. I have many more guidelines you'll have picked up from within this book, and yes, they are important in your business-buying decision, but the following seven rules are imperative.

To put this really simply, the only time I've lost in business is when I broken my own set of rules … so, be prepared to follow each and every one of them, and keep them close by so it's easy for you.

The only reason most people fail in the money game is they get far too greedy. They'd rather get this deal to show how good they are at negotiation or something similar, rather than waiting to do a good deal that meets all the rules.

Remember, walk away from more deals than you take.  NOT doing a deal never killed anyone.

## RULE #1 … Surviving Despite Itself

Ever walked into a shop where you were literally amazed at how badly they did things?  The service was bad, the shop was dirty, the people didn't seem to care, and yet somehow, despite all this they seemed to be making money.

I call this my "Idiot Rule".  In other words, I want to buy the business from someone who has no idea what they are doing, no idea how to sell, serve or even do the numbers.  I want to buy the business from an idiot.

I know this seems awful, but the fact is, if they're not even doing the absolutely common sense stuff, then when I buy it, the business will get increased sales just because I will.

Somehow, even with the bad service, bad skill-set, almost bad everything, they're making enough money to get by. It could be something as simple as a great location that keeps them going.  You know, they're the only supplier in town – that kind of thing.

It could be the product or service they sell is in such demand that no matter what they do people would still buy from them.  Exclusive dealerships seem to fit this category.

A couple of things you'll want to be sure to look for.  The team, or as they're more commonly known – the staff, don't want to be there. You'll probably have to sack about half the current people, so you don't have to put up with the same bad attitudes pervading the business when you own it.

A hint here: I prefer to have the previous owner let go of the entire staff, pay out all superannuation, long service leave, holiday pay and so on, then I re-hire the team members I want.

One last point here. Low customer satisfaction is almost guaranteed, so be sure to let past customers know there has been a drastic change of management.

## RULE #2 ... Cashflow NOT Assets

Remember earlier I stated that, for me, Business is for Cashflow and Property is for Assets. So when I'm buying a business I'm buying a cashflow stream, not a heavily asset-laden company.

I don't want to tie my money up in the hard assets of a business. Nor do I care to worry about large amounts of depreciation and replacing plant and equipment.

You see, first and foremost in business I want a RETURN ON INVESTMENT with the Profits from the cashflow, not just the ultimate increase in Capital Value. Unfortunately, most business owners have been lead to believe the equity they're building is enough reason to keep running a business. NOT TRUE ...

You've got to be collecting cash profits over and above your wages along the way to make it all worthwhile.

Usually this rule will restrict you to the more service, wholesale and retail type of businesses rather than manufacturing businesses. That's not to say you can't make money in manufacturing, it's just it's easier to get a massive increase in sales with a service, wholesale or retail business.

Remember, business is cashflow, property is an asset. That's why I recommend you shouldn't directly be your own landlord. There are only two ways I'll buy both a property and a business together. The first is if there's a way I can sell either the property or the business and get back the cash I invested up front straight away.

For example, you might buy a freehold shop and sell the shop for cash to make the down payment back straight away. Thus, you own the building with a loan and no cash down. You've also got a good tenant whose lease you negotiate before you sell.

Or, you could sell off the building and keep the business, so you own the business outright with no cash of your own after the sale of the building goes through at a profit on your purchase.

The second way is to buy the building through your investment company or trust and the business totally separately. That way you are your Landlord, but not really.

One last thing to stress here: the end sale price is irrelevant when you're considering buying a business. The most important part here is … can you make a positive cashflow or profit from the business in the meantime? Then you can also make a great profit from the final sale.

Remember the basics; business is for cashflow, and shares and property are for assets.

## RULE #3 … Low Skills and a Staple Product or Service

This has got to be one of the most often broken rules. But perhaps more importantly, it's also one of the simplest rules to stick with. And, here's why …

Firstly, let's deal with the low skill type business. Put simply, I don't want to buy an architects firm. It's not that I have anything against architects in particular; it's just they're highly skilled, highly paid, highly trained, and in most cases, they want to be paid a lot more than is economically viable.

I want a business where the people I employ are easy to hire, easy to train, won't cost me a lot, and are relatively easy to keep. I'd prefer to run an advertisement for a vacant position and get 100 responses to choose from, rather than receiving just a few.

I'd rather invest just a day or two training new people on how to run the systems than a month on all of the refined skills needed in a high-skill business. And, I'd rather hire people who have a mortgage to pay, and kids to take care of and who want a long-term, secure position in my company.

In fact, one of the best groups to hire is people who've tried to run their own business and failed. They're willing to work hard and yet know the risks of the business are no longer theirs. These people make the best General Managers.

Secondly, let's look at the 'staple product or service' idea ...

Far too often I get the 'I invented something new' crowd at my seminars. Remember, you may think you can make a better burger than McDonalds, but can you make a better business and marketing system?

Couple this with the fact it's far easier to grab your share of an already baked pie, than it is to go out, grow the ingredients, create a brand new recipe and then eventually get the pie cooked, after you build a new stove.

Basically what I'm trying to say in my own very long-winded way is I want to sell a product or service people already know they need, and their buying decision is only 'WHO, will I buy it from?' and not 'SHOULD I buy it at all?' These I call the STAPLE BUYS – the walk in and walk out type of purchases we make all the time. They involve low cost, multiple purchase products that we simply can't do without. They are the things we NEED to buy, not the things we just WANT to buy.

I love to sell to people who have to buy this product or service anyway; they just have to decide if they'll buy it from my competitor or me. To put it simply, I remove any thoughts of a competitor because I just do it better.

I think it would be easier to help people succeed if they only knew that instead of a new invention, they should … SELL SHOES …

Everybody already wears shoes, they already buy them, it's just a matter of which pair, and from which store …

If I haven't already made this so very clear … don't invent something new … just sell what people already want to buy.

There is one thing you need to be inventive about though …you need to invent a much better way of doing business - new sales systems, new marketing systems, new customer service strategies, new operational systems, and so on. Build a better business model, not a better product or service.

Remember, it's not just what you sell; it's how you sell it.

## RULE #4 … Bad Sales and Marketing

I once had one of my clients ask me if I would buy her business after we'd created great marketing and sales systems for her team. Of course my answer was a firm – NO.

You want them to have been doing some marketing and advertising, but you want them to be doing really bad stuff. How bad you ask? Bad enough that with just a little common sense you can get a much better result.

Even not-so-good customer service is OK. When you change things, you'll make a massive difference. In fact, if their store is dirty, their brochures really bad, their uniforms all faded and so on, you should celebrate. Not just because they'll be easy to fix, but also because you already have a list of what needs to change in order to get the company more profitable before you buy it.

So, here's what I recommend. Read my earlier books, 'Instant Cashflow' and 'Cash, Customers and Ads that Sell' if you really want to get a hold on these principles of making more money through great marketing.

Also, you want to ask them about how well their ads work, and whether they produce a response.

"Oh, I'm not sure, they seem to be OK". This is a sure fire sign you can make a few simple changes to get great results.

Make sure they've done no real measuring of results from their marketing. Of course, you will be testing and measuring everything when you buy the business, but you want to make sure they have no idea what worked and what didn't.

Maybe they've kept a list of past customers but have never used it. With any luck, they'll have entered them onto a database for you, but even if they only had business cards or old order forms, it's best for you if they've never used their database for anything other than sending out invoices.

Hopefully for you (though not for me) they've never read my books, attended my seminars or used any of the simple sales, marketing and business building strategies I teach in them.

This will leave you with lots of great marketing opportunities that won't cost you much. I love a business where they've been spending $1,000 or more per week from their marketing budget but in reality never really added a cent to the bottom line.

I can either divert this money into great advertising or pocket it as pure profit every week. Remember, poor marketing is a sign of a great opportunity for you.

## RULE #5 ... Hire a Great Jockey

It amazes me how many people start a business that specializes in the line of work they have some level of expertise in. Firstly because they start it from scratch, and secondly because they work as an employee in the business instead of as the owner of the business. This, of course, wastes twice as much of their time as doing what I'm recommending here.

One of the best ways I find to decide what business I'm going to buy next is to meet the right person who'll run the business for me. You know what I mean, when you find just the right person to run it. It could be that you met a great waiter or chef or barkeeper so you buy a bar and restaurant.

It could be you met a great hairdresser, so you buy a salon ... you get the picture.

Now, at the start you will most probably be your own jockey for two reasons. Firstly so you can learn how to build businesses, and second so you can preserve capital. There are a lot of things to learn about growing a company, and to put it very simply, there's no way to learn them other than to do it yourself.

Basically, you'll use your time capital to build up your reserves of cash capital. If however, you're blessed with a stack of cash you may decide to start by hiring a good jockey right from the first business you build.

I think I really need to stress to you this is the most important of these seven rules. Here's why ...

If you were to consider the best race horse ever to run a lap on a race track, how well do you think it would run if you had a big, fat, heavy, six foot tall jockey who'd only ever ridden donkeys for fun?

Of course it would run last. The same is true for a business; a great business can still be killed by a bad jockey.

So, what's a great jockey look like?

There are probably five things you'd want to find in every jockey you hire.

**Number 1.** They take responsibility for what goes on in the business. In fact they act as if they own it. You may even like to give them a 10 or 20% share in the business if they meet certain goals one or two years into the business' growth.

**Number 2.** They have owned their own business in the past and either sold it for a small profit or shut it down and decided they'd rather work for someone else.

**Number 3.** They're a great DO'er. In other words, they love to get in there and do the work rather than sit back and come up with ideas. That's your job. You want someone who will do the work and lead the team for you, while you're playing golf.

**Number 4.** They have a great deal of experience in the industry you're going in to. Just because I told you I don't think you should buy a business where you know what you're doing, doesn't mean you shouldn't hire someone who does.

**Number 5.** They're honest. I know it seems simple enough, but the number of business owners I've met who've lost money by not doing a simple reference check is amazing.

Remember, in business, you back a great jockey first and then you find a great horse for the jockey to ride ...

## RULE #6 ... High Upside

Put simply, if you can't get a lot of improvement, you can't make a lot of money. Any business you buy shouldn't be anywhere near running at its full capacity. For example, if you're buying a hairdressing salon and they have five cutting stations and five full-time hairdressers, one always at every station, then they're running at capacity, thus there's no upside.

I would never buy this business, as there's no real room for growth. Of course, where we make our money is on growing the business so it's now worth a whole lot more than before.

One thing you might like to keep in mind; the business can be making a loss when you buy it. Not a big loss every week, but a small loss. Obviously, this small loss makes it easier to convince the seller to give you the business for no money down.

One thing I will add here though. If you're buying a loss-making business, you'd better be very clear on exactly what needs to be done to turn it into a profitable business inside the first month.

In other words, it has to be able to make a profit, and make it very quickly. On that, what amount of profit can the company make per month? If its total monthly profit limit (when it's at 90 to 100% of capacity) is maybe only $3,000 a month, is it really worth the effort?

I like to look for at minimum a $10,000 a month-type business. This gives me a good solid business to sell and allows me to sell the business somewhere in the $100,000 to $500,000 bracket. What I aim for is usually a good saleable price, with enough potential buyers (the number doesn't need to be that large) to sell reasonably quickly in most markets.

So, a rule of thumb, buy a business that seems to be running at about 25% of it's capacity and put it back on the market when you've got it running at about 75% of capacity. This way you leave enough room for growth for the next person to see themselves already with a profit, but with still some room to get more.

By the way, this could mean increasing revenues by more than 10 times. Just because people are working at 25%, doesn't mean they're making any money. It takes the same level of work to open the office everyday and make no money as it does to make just enough to get by.

So, 50% of growth in capacity from 25% to 75% doesn't always mean only a 300% growth (25% x 3 = 75%) in revenues.

One last thing; a high upside could also mean a business you can get for no money down and sell for a still rock-bottom price only weeks later with tens of thousands in profits. Remember; look for the high upside every time.

## RULE #7 ... Great Deal

This is probably the most obvious rule of all, but because of emotions, it rarely gets followed. Ever been to a house auction and seen the other people get carried away with the fun, excitement and desire to win at all costs. I'm assuming it's never been you who got carried away with your emotions and paid far too much for something 'you just HAD to have.'

Set your price before you walk in the door. In fact, before you walk out of your own door you should have a firm price in mind. And whatever happens, NEVER EVER pay more than that price.

Now, this might mean a negotiation takes months and months and in MOST cases it'll mean you don't do a deal.

Write this as a note to yourself ...

SELF – Walk away from more deals than you take ...

Don't renegotiate. This isn't an auction or a game you have to win at all costs. It's a transaction whereby the person selling has only a few interested parties, if that.

And the person buying ... YOU ... has at least a hundred more opportunities to look at next week and then the next week and then the next week again.

A good friend of mine puts it's best. He says: "The deal of the century comes along every week".

Your terms should include several subject to's before the deal will go through. The most common ones I use are these ...

Subject to partner's approval.

Subject to accountants' inspection.

Subject to hiring a good 'jockey'. Of course you use the title of the position you want filled instead of the word 'jockey'.

Subject to vendor finance for $X over Y period of time at Z interest rate.

Subject to ... almost anything you want ...

One way to know you're making a deal that will be profitable for you in the long run is to know the seller had to take a cash LOSS. That's right, if they make a profit from what they paid compared to the price you're offering, then you've just forfeited a chunk of the profit you should receive when you eventually sell the business.

If they're not hurting when they do the deal, you've probably given up too much. More on this in a few pages ...

In fact, you should make your own rule that your first deal has to be No Money Down. Remember, you're investing so make it a great deal and only buy if it's on your terms and meets all the rules.

## Doing the Deal

Put simply, this is where you will make or break yourself and your path to super riches. I have to stress the importance of every step of this process, but especially right here where you get to do the deal.

For most, the whole negotiation process is an emotional roller coaster filled with excitement, fear, panic, stress and either celebration or commiseration. It's controlling these emotions and the many more you're likely to feel and express that is vital in doing a great deal.

In a moment we'll look in depth at the emotions you'll experience and how to deal with them, but suffice to say, impatience is the biggest killer of them all. If I love my negotiation opponents to have just one emotional flaw, it would be that of impatience. I can always out-wait a seller and remember, I'm happy to walk away from any and every deal.

By the way, my Mum doesn't like me talking about things like this. She thinks I'm mean and nasty. She thinks I take advantage of people, and she's probably right; I take advantage of the fact I'm smarter than most, I know how to fix their business and they don't. I take advantage of the fact I don't need to do a deal, yet most people I deal with do. And, I take advantage of the fact every human being has choice, especially the choice to say NO to me.

That's why I keep stressing; "this is business." And, I make my profit when I buy the business, so I had better be darn good at it.

One last point that's vitally important; negotiate slowly, but when you get a figure, do the deal quickly.

## Negotiation

This important negotiation point I've just mentioned really makes sense when you understand people's emotions. People want to get a deal done, and in the end they just give up.

They'd rather have the pain of a cash loss than the pain of running their business for another day. Remember, a shopkeeper will sell old stock below cost just to get rid of it.

Negotiation is a fun and tricky game of flexibility. You see, the person who's most flexible and cares the least about doing the deal usually wins.

To make sure you negotiate well, here are some hints and tips.

Firstly, deal with ALL decision makers at first and then only deal with the one person who will be the true decision maker as you progress. In many businesses you'll be faced with a husband and wife partnership, but ultimately only one of them will make the decision and you need to work out which one that is.

Secondly, to do this you may want to take negotiation classes. It's the fastest way to get others to enjoy giving you what you want. Let me cover that again, because it's vitally important. Negotiation is the communicative art form that gets people to enjoy giving you what you want.

Break that down and what's it tell you. You have to master communication, you have to be able to read people and you have to be clear on what you want. Some of these skills will come naturally; others you'll have to work on.

Thirdly, if you want to make it in the business of buying, building and selling businesses, you've got to get tough. You can't just do a deal because you feel sorry for someone. You're going to meet a lot of people who've put themselves into bad financial and emotional positions out there.

You can't pay extra just because you 'really want this one'. When I say tough, what I truly mean is tough with yourself. Only allow yourself to do the deal if it's on your terms. The terms you wrote down before you entered into negotiation.

Sellers often have tactics too. One such tactic is called the take away close; it's where you take the deal away from the prospective buyer and almost show them that they're not allowed to buy. In negotiation it's all about saying 'NO' first. Never get into a position whereby you let the seller say no to you, always get yourself into a position of power by saying no and walking away. Give them time - many will call you back.

Think of it as being no different from a bartering situation in an Asian or South American market place. You would have no hesitation in walking away from a stallholder if your offer wasn't accepted, wouldn't you?

Now for the last point I want to make on the subject of negotiation. It is up to you to SELL them the deal. You've got to sell yourself, sell your abilities and sell them on the fact the deal you bring is the best deal they'll get.

As an example, let's just say I was looking at a residential property to invest in. As I own a lot of these already, let me show you what generally happens. The Realtor usually sells the owner on taking an offer, or tells them not to take it as they think they can get more for it.

If all I did was tell the agent how much I loved the house, but I just didn't think it was worth anywhere near what they were asking, the agent would sell the owner on the fact the 'The Market' is telling them it's not worth what we estimated and they think you should accept the offer.

When you're negotiating on a business, you generally won't have an agent so you'll have to do the agents work yourself. Remember, negotiate long and tough, and most importantly, stay with your original offer.

## Emotions – Fall in Love with the Deal, NOT the Business

It's a fatal mistake to believe the business you've just found is the perfect one for you. It seems as if it's meant to be, you think. You've clicked with the seller and in any case you've always dreamt of owning such a business. You just knew the opportunity would crop up one day, so this must be it.

Remember this; there are a million and one deals out there. If this one doesn't come together, there are thousands more from which to choose this month.

Don't fall into the trap of being taken in by the setting, the physical appearance of the business, or the décor. Don't fall in love with the drapes. These are all emotional factors. In fact, tell yourself you will change everything anyway.

One of my prime rules is: Forget the business, love the deal. It's the deal you're after, not the fact you've always wanted to own a florist shop. The intention isn't to buy yourself a job, but a business.

Get the sellers to love you. You need to sell yourself. Once you have them liking and believing in you, they will find themselves trusting you. They will be more open to listening to your ideas and suggestions. And to your eventual offer.

But you need to remember you must remain tough, especially on yourself. You are there for a purpose, and it is a business purpose. You must make sure you leave your emotions at home.

When you're there in front of sellers, think of yourself as an actor. You are trying to portray yourself as a likeable person, a go-getter who will run the business well and who will succeed. Business owners, like property owners, do like knowing their business is passing on into good hands. You see, owners tend to think of their business on an emotional level. Some of the more likely emotions you'll encounter include scarcity, impatience, fear and excitement. More often than not they have built the business up themselves; it's their baby. You need to convince them the deal you are offering is the absolute best they'll get, and you need to come across as honest and sincere. You want them to feel, at the end of the day, they have done as well as could be expected.

## Walking Away

If there's one skill you need to master in the art of negotiation, it's to be able to walk away. In fact, you need to be able to RUN.

I know you may be thinking this sounds a bit odd. Why would you want to approach a seller only to be prepared to run away? Isn't the object of the exercise to stay negotiating?

Consider this: Of every ten businesses you look at, only between one and three will get to the negotiation stage. That means you should say NO to nine out of ten deals.

You see, what you are essentially doing here is shaking the tree to see what falls out. If you shake long and hard enough, eventually something will.

## Someone Must take a CASH Loss

Now I know what we've all been taught. I know the textbooks say we should be aiming for a WIN-WIN situation. This is one of the biggest fallacies when it comes to negotiating the sale of a business.

There are other 'wins' sellers can have through the sale of their business. They can get on with the rest of their lives. They can go forward without the weight of a lease on their premises to worry about. You're saving their Butt.

One other thing; if your offer is so low that, in the eyes of the seller they are making an unacceptable loss, it might still be more palatable than continuing on indefinitely with a loss-making business. You see, even though it might be a bitter pill to swallow, a perpetual loss is more hurtful than taking a once-off loss now.

Remember, sellers can always say NO to your offer. The choice is theirs.

Remember too, when you are the buyer, you are in the driving seat. The initiative should always be yours. Don't loose it. You are only responsible for yourself.

**The Profit is in the Purchase**

This is one of the least understood principles of buying a business. The profit you make when buying a business is at the time of purchase, not when you eventually sell it.

You can only sell at a profit if you buy at a loss. Not your loss, the seller's. Remember, somebody has to be loosing through the sale of a business. Your job is to ensure it's not you. If you give in to the seller's demands during negotiation, you are contributing to their success.

Another thing most people fail to realize is you get your money back from cashflow, not from the sale price when you eventually sell. And every extra dollar you pay when you buy means another $10 or even $100 in cashflow you'll have to generate.

# Building the Business

This is the area I find scares most people off. Yet it is really simple. Once you understand what I am about to teach you, you will be absolutely amazed.

But before I go any further, I will point out it is assumed you'll be operating at Level 4. And it is at this level you will benefit most from having a Business Coach to lead you and to encourage you along your road to riches.

I'd also like to point out that by playing my board game LEVERAGE, and by reading my books Instant Cashflow, and Cash, Customers, And Ads That Sell you will become familiar with all the tools you will ever need to grow your business beyond your wildest dreams.

What I am now going to teach you is the NUMBER ONE, the MOST IMPORTANT thing you'll ever learn about business – ever.

How do I know this? I've taught it to hundreds of thousands of people and every time the answer is the same – "WOW, that's amazing!"

Let me start this way: Many years ago Ferdinand Porsche used the Volkswagen Beetle chassis to build his first sports car. Most people in business don't understand there is a CHASSIS that is the central theme of business, and because they don't understand it they tend to drive Volkswagens and not Porsches. The moment you understand what I am about to teach you, you'll always be driving a Porsche business rather than a Volkswagen business.  Your business will grow at the rate of a Porsche and not a Volkswagen.

## The Five Ways

There are only FIVE things you need to do to grow a business. Only five. And you need to do them simultaneously. It's a bit like going to the gym and only working on the muscles in your left arm for a week, then working on your right arm the week thereafter, and so on. That's ridiculous.

Here's the formula:

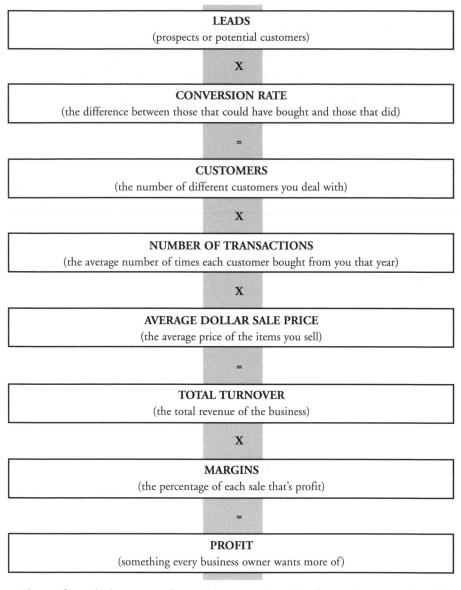

**LEADS**
(prospects or potential customers)

X

**CONVERSION RATE**
(the difference between those that could have bought and those that did)

=

**CUSTOMERS**
(the number of different customers you deal with)

X

**NUMBER OF TRANSACTIONS**
(the average number of times each customer bought from you that year)

X

**AVERAGE DOLLAR SALE PRICE**
(the average price of the items you sell)

=

**TOTAL TURNOVER**
(the total revenue of the business)

X

**MARGINS**
(the percentage of each sale that's profit)

=

**PROFIT**
(something every business owner wants more of)

I have found there are three things, and only three, that people who come to me for help, need help on. They are customers, turnover, and profit. Notice how these are all things that follow the equal signs in the formula above. They are all the result of something else in the formula.

Understand this: If you want to change a result, you have to change what goes into it. You can't make a better cake with the same recipe. You need to change the variables – in our case the leads, the conversion rate, the number of transactions, the average $ sale price, and the margins.

These are the only five things you need to do to grow your business.

Now, let's look at an example. I've inserted some simple figures into our formula.

| |
|---|
| **LEADS** <br> 4,000 |

X

| |
|---|
| **CONVERSION RATE** <br> 25% |

=

| |
|---|
| **CUSTOMERS** <br> 1,000 |

X

| |
|---|
| **NUMBER OF TRANSACTIONS** <br> 2 |

X

| |
|---|
| **AVERAGE DOLLAR SALE PRICE** <br> 100 |

=

| |
|---|
| **TOTAL TURNOVER** <br> 200,000 |

X

| |
|---|
| **MARGINS** <br> 25% |

=

| |
|---|
| **PROFIT** <br> 50,000 |

Now, having read my book Instant Cashflow, in which I give you 60 ways to generate more leads, 58 ways to boost your conversion rate, 50 strategies for boosting your number of transactions, 49 ways to boost your average dollar sale, and 65 ways to boost your margins, do you think you can achieve just a 10% increase the variables in our formula? Of course you can. It's dead easy!

Now, let's rework the formula (with only a 10% increase in the figures.)

| LEADS |
|:---:|
| 4,400 |

X

| CONVERSION RATE |
|:---:|
| 27.5% |

=

| CUSTOMERS |
|:---:|
| 1,210 |

X

| NUMBER OF TRANSACTIONS |
|:---:|
| 2.2 |

X

| AVERAGE DOLLAR SALE PRICE |
|:---:|
| 110 |

=

| TOTAL TURNOVER |
|:---:|
| 292,820 |

X

| MARGINS |
|:---:|
| 27.5% |

=

| PROFIT |
|:---:|
| 80,525.50 |

I want you to notice something here; for just a 10% increase in the five variables, we get a 46% increase in total turnover and a whopping 61% increase in profit. And people have told me you can only increase profit by 10% a year. What nonsense! Anyone whose business isn't growing massively obviously doesn't realize they should be driving a Porsche, not a Volkswagen.

The chassis works, no matter what business you're in. Don't even bother telling me you can't grow your business.

So, let's now look at a few other areas in your business you should address during the building phase.

## Systems

When building your business, one of the basic aims you will have is to build it so it runs smoothly WITHOUT you. For this to happen, you need to develop and implement good systems. You want to stop the business running you and start running your business.

You need to build your systems so they can cater for all eventualities. They need to be able to cope with both the routine as well as the exceptional. And when a problem arises, your team needs only to look to the system for answers.

With good systems in place, you should be able to put your business on automatic pilot. Then you won't have to be there day in, day out, week in, week out, month-by-month, year-by-year. Impossible? Visit my web site www.actionplanning.tv to find out more about the AutoPilot[a] system. You see, one of the disruptive influences in business is dealing with the unknown – attending to things like putting out fires each day and always working on the immediate problem at hand. This does not allow you to create long-term viability... rather it traps you in your business for years and years. If you have ever felt there must be a better way, there is. AutoPilot™ has been specifically designed to help create stability within your business so you can get on with the important things like building wealth and creating more freedom of choice.

A good place to start when developing your systems is to list all routine, daily, weekly or monthly activities each employee needs to do. That will give you a very good idea of the flow of information or activity within the business. You could do this by writing down these activities. You could also photograph them, or capture them on video or audiotape.

You'll be mapping out the various positions within the business according to the activities they perform. This will also assist you when you come to write Position Descriptions. You'll also be allocating Key Performance Indicators (KPI's) for each position so you can appraise each person's performance from time to time.

What you're basically doing here is laying the foundation for the success of your business. Think of it as setting the direction for the future growth and prosperity of your business, and yourself.

You need to take a good hard look at all that is needed when it comes to managing your business. Write everything down so one day, if you're not there, someone could do it just as well. Create a Management Manual – a step-by-step guide.

Next, concentrate on listing all the things you do to create interest in your product and service. Make sure everything is covered so anyone could step in if needed to perform these tasks. Do the same for sales.

How you provide your valuable exchangeable product also needs to be covered in detail. Other areas you should systematize in this way include how you develop your people, your cash systems, steps to be taken to reduce downtime, and how the business can be run from a distance.

When you've done this, you'll end up with a complete system manual for your business. And it'll be a living document; encourage your people to keep it that way by introducing changes and improvements whenever possible.

## Marketing

There are truly only five ways to multiply your business profits. Remember the Business Chassis? You'll need to develop a Marketing Plan to ensure everyone in your business works together towards achieving common goals. To do this they need to know where they're heading in a marketing sense. They need to know what the goals are, whom their target market is, what to do to generate more leads, and whether what they are already doing is working.

Marketing Plans can be as simple or as detailed as you like, but they should all contain information that is designed to address the five basic parts you can influence in the Business Chassis. Let's take a quick look at each of them.

**Lead Generation.** The marketing plan should outline how the business will generate new business leads. There are many ways in which this can be done. These include newspaper advertisements, television advertisements, radio advertisements, industry newsletter advertisements, inserts, press releases, sidewalk handbills, brochures, catalogues, direct mail, fax outs, sponsorships, window displays and even competitions. There are many, many more ways that could be considered.

**Conversion Rate.** One of the problems most businesses face is converting prospective customers into customers. How do you entice someone who walks into your shop to kill time before his or her bus arrives, to make a purchase? How do you make sure a prospective customer buys from you and not the store down the road? Your marketing plan needs to address this issue. Some of the techniques it could detail include providing a written guarantee, developing your own unique product line, running offers and special promotions, offering a mail order service, training the team in sales, providing a first buyer's incentive, or offering a gift cheque towards a purchase.

**Number of Transactions.** Hanging on to an existing customer is far easier, and much cheaper, than looking for new ones. Therefore, this is one area that needs to be concentrated on in the marketing plan. How do you ensure those customers you have make repeat purchases? How do you get them to buy more from you? Useful techniques include making your customers feel extra special, under promising and over delivering, keeping in regular contact with them, never running out of stock, pre-selling or taking pre-payments, accepting trade-ins, suggesting alternative uses for products they show interest in, holding closed door sales and offering free trials.

**Average Dollar Sale.** Increasing your average dollar sale is another very important, yet easily achievable, element that must be covered in your marketing plan. Some ideas on how to do this include increasing your prices across the board, up-selling your customers or upgrading their purchases, add-on selling, carrying point of sale material, or offering customer incentives for bigger purchases.

**Margin.** Your margins can be increased by concentrating on selling higher priced items, selling an exclusive label, selling through the internet, reducing the amount of overtime you pay, consider allowing some staff to work from home, renting out idle space, and keeping overheads to a minimum.

One quick point here: Most people tell me they want more customers. They simply can't get that. What they can get is get more leads and an improvement in their conversion rate. Similarly, you can't get more turnover. Get it? You need to address the variables that result in a higher turnover.

It's important to note business consists of two equally important parts; marketing and distribution. The challenge is most business owners put about 90% of their effort into distribution and only 10% into marketing. You've got to market if you're ever going to make real money.

The basic aim of the marketing plan is to help you MULTIPLY your business profits, not to ADD to them.

As mentioned earlier, there are only five ways to grow your business. To do that, concentrate on the BUSINESS CHASSIS.

## Team Building

Imagine the people you're about to lead each being represented by a massive 16-cylinder engine. Ask yourself how many cylinders each person is currently running on. Some will be running on four, some on eight. Now, in order to get each and every one of them running on all 16, we need to understand how human beings are built.

We all have four main segments; body, mind, heart and spirit.

The average organization only considers the first two when hiring people. Some even tell you to leave your emotional stuff at home. It's very important to understand body and mind only have, in my analogy, three cylinders each. These are the sorts of things you read about people on people's resumes. But if you think about it, the more important things are heart and spirit, which, in my analogy have five cylinders each. They are the attributes that tell you whether a person has the drive, the passion and the get-up-and-go for the job.

When you have people firing on all 16 cylinders, you'll be absolutely amazed at the results. This is because there will now be synergy in the team. Understand this; the synergy in a team is one of the things that will jump your business to a level you never expected.

So, how do you build a winning team?

1. There's no substitute for strong leadership. Little can usually be achieved without the co-operation of others. As a leader, you must create excellent people in your business. You must help them to grow so your business can grow. Keep their knowledge updated, and work harder on yourself than on your job. Remember, you always get the people you deserve. Become a great leader and you will get great people. Learn to think outside the square. Walk the walk, don't just talk the talk.

2. The next thing you need to do is to set a common goal. You need to tell every member of your team what the goal of your business is. You can't expect them to achieve results if they don't know what the overall goal is that they must be aiming for.

3. You must set the rules of the game. You must tell them what they can, and can't, do. You need to create the playing field. Everyone must know the rules, which must be written down and available. You see, if you don't give them the rules, they'll go outside the boundaries.

4. You need an action plan. The first thing you need to do here is to give everyone a position description. They need to know what their job entails and their responsibilities are. The second thing you need to do is to develop a strategy that lays down how results are to be achieved and why certain things are done. Thirdly, you need a tactic, which spells out how results will be achieved. You then need to develop systems by which your team can achieve results, and you need to tell them who is doing what by when. You see, part of playing in a championship team is making sure you stay in position. After all, that is what you are accountable for, isn't it? This doesn't mean if someone asks for help, you don't give it. It means you come to a resolution so you can still get on with your job while assisting them in finding a solution to their problem.

5. You must be willing to take risks. If you don't, the team will always lag behind and will not push boundaries.

6. You need to make sure everyone on the team has involvement. And this involvement must be 100% by 100% of the team. They all need to be firing on all 16 cylinders.

7. You must practice the art of inclusion. Let me talk about sabotage to illustrate this point. If someone is trying to sabotage your organization covertly, they can easily do so just by not getting involved in the work situation. You can counter this by asking for their opinion and then listening to what they say. If, on the other hand, they wanted to sabotage your business overtly, they can do this by taking control. This is the biggest single stumbling block in team situations.

While on the topic of control, consider this: If the owners of a business thinks they needs to control everything, they will eventually loose control as it's impossible to control anything but yourself. Their controlling tendencies will destroy the business. As business owners, we must ask ourselves how do we run a business if we can't control it.

People are amazing – they will achieve extraordinary results when you let them. The people you work with can be far more effective if you create an environment where each of you helps the other create synergy. Without the people who can run the business, you'll trap yourself in the business forever. I train my people to be better than me.

Remember, you can train your people and loose a few, or not train them and loose the business.

## Customer Service

Customer service is a cliché, if ever there was one. And it must be one of the most misconstrued concepts in business today. The name of the game is making customer service PAY. It never ceases to amaze me how most businesses go about tackling the question of customer service. What most of them do is to start by spending large amounts of money in an attempt to impress their customers. What they fail to do is to find out if this will make them any more money or not. You see, great customer service without bottom line results is a waste of time and money.

Let me now share with you the three steps you must take to achieving great, and meaningful, customer service.

**Step # 1.** You must aim for CONSISTENCY. It's no good if whatever you do differs each day. Your customers will want to know that whenever they visit your business the service will be the same. And it doesn't matter what the level of customer service is, so long as it's consistent. I mean if you are running a five star hotel you will serve your dinner guests at their tables, whereas if you were running a fast food outlet you wouldn't. This doesn't mean the customer service at the fast food joint is inferior to that at the hotel. It would just be different; at a different level. And you must offer consistency in both service and delivery.

**Step #2.** Make it EASY for customers TO BUY. You see, with consistency comes TRUST. By building consistency into your sales process, you will ensure you systematically surpass their expectations every time they buy from you. They will begin to trust your business; they will know every time they buy from you there will be no unpleasant surprises. They receive the same pleasant greeting each and every time they arrive, they receive the same efficient and courteous service while they are there and their questions are answered accurately and honestly. Do everything possible to make their buying experience easy. This way, they will know what to expect when they return next time.

**Step #3.** Now do the WOW. This is the way to create raving fans. Understand this: the fundamentals of creating great customer service involve creating a system to make sure your customer's expectations are surpassed, every time. Having satisfied customers implies you have given them all they've wanted, but nothing more. But if you're going to surpass their expectations, you must systematically go beyond their expectations. Every single day you need to be getting better. The Japanese have a good term for this. They call it Kaisen – constant and never ending improvement.

To do this, you need to go further than just providing great customer service. You need to implement a customer service plan, which comprises the following action points:

1. Identify your ideal customers. Find out who they are.

2. Create your customer service vision. Remember, customer service is about understanding the little things are important. You need to make an impression on your customers.

3. Conduct market research. You need to ask your ideal customers what they would regard as excellent customer service.

4. Now create your customers' customer service vision.

5. Take the two visions and combine them to create an ultimate customer service vision.

6. Decide what it is you can promise your customers. This must be something you can deliver each and every time. My rule is to under promise and over deliver.

7. Make sure you get your team involved. Give them the vision, and ask them for ideas on how it can be delivered. Work consistently with them on this.

8. Make sure you have continual check-ups. Make sure you are delivering what you promise.

9. As your level of service gets better, move the goal posts. Keep improving.

10. Always give your customers more than they expect. I send out free gifts continually.

11. And always smile. You see, people love to feel special.

People are willing to PAY for service - when it's the service they desire. If the service exceeds their expectations, they will STAY with you and they will SAY good things about your business.

But if your service is poor, they'll WALK away, they'll TALK negatively about your business, and they'll BAULK at coming back.

Be consistent, always smile and give your customer's more than they expect. And be sure they leave with a smile on their face.

Most good businesses spend time and money in the pursuit of good customer service so they can get customers to come back and make further purchases. But understand good customer service in itself doesn't build customer loyalty. Take, as an example, two businesses. One gives average customer service and the other prides itself on its good customer service. If the first business writes a follow-up letter to its customers inviting them to shop there again whereas the second one doesn't, where do you think the customers are more likely to shop next? At the first business, even though its customer service is rated as only being average.

OK, so let's take a closer look at this very important concept – customer loyalty.

How do you build loyal customers? I like to explain this using the loyalty ladder concept. What I mean by this is you have to move your customers up this ladder, and you need to keep them moving up the ladder all the time. Think of it just like an ordinary ladder. If you were to step up onto the first rung of the ladder, would you just hang around there for a while before doing something? No, you would want to climb up straight away, or get off.

Now, ask yourself why it is you want to build a loyalty ladder for your business. I'd suggest it is because the first sale you make to a customer is made at a loss. Yes, statistics show nine out of ten first sales are made at a loss, because there are advertising costs, marketing costs and commissions that first need to be taken into account. If you don't get that customer to come back and buy again, that customer isn't profitable to you.

Let's now take a closer look at the loyalty ladder and what the various stages on it involve:

## Raving Fan

| Advocate |
| Member |
| Customer |
| Shopper |
| Prospect |
| Suspect |

1. **SUSPECT.** When they first start out on the loyalty ladder, right at the bottom rung, people are called suspects. How do you identify them? They are only potential customers at this stage, they fit within your target market and they are willing to buy from you if they are in your geographic area.

2. **PROSPECT.** We then move up the ladder to prospect. A prospect is a suspect who has taken some sort of action like phoning in off an ad or visiting your business. You must collect all their details so you can stay in touch. This is most important, as building customer loyalty is all about relationship building. You will be aiming to build a database of prospects. You now use all your sales skills to move your prospect one rung up the ladder to the next stage, to that of customer.

3. **CUSTOMER.** To be classified as a customer, your prospect needs to have spent money, and you need to have recorded the sale in your records. This last step may seem strange, but it is most important, because it allows you to differentiate between prospects and customers on your database. You see, if you are planning to send a letter out to all prospects offering them an incentive to buy, you don't want to be sending it to people who are already customers. This record will also tell you when they last bought, how often they buy and what their average dollar sale is. Here's something you'll find interesting: I find most businesses put up a huge STOP sign at this level. The salespeople seem to sit back waiting for these customers to return, instead of taking proactive action and inviting them back. Understand at the customer level, they have cost you money. If you are content to stop at this level, your business will eventually go broke. I have eaten out at many restaurants, and guess what? I'm not on any database. I've never received a letter from any of them saying: "Brad, we'd love to have you back." This is, to my mind, quite insane. They seem to be saying; "You've bought, now I'm going to just hope like heck you come back." Think about the possibilities for your business. The STOP sign is the scariest thing I've come across in business. You need to get rid of it, and fast.

4. **MEMBER.** When your customers make their second purchase, they become members. They now have a feeling of belonging. Understand customers who make two purchases are ten times more likely to make more than someone who has only made one. So, you need to put some

effort into your members. Give them a membership card and a membership pack. How many of your customers know all your products? Very few, I would suggest. So why not include a product catalogue in the membership pack? You can also include samples, vouchers and things like that. One interesting example I came across recently was at a truck stop in New Zealand. The owner pinned up photographs on a notice board of all drivers who had stopped the night there. Then there's the coffee shop that gives you your own personalized coffee mug. Each time you come in, they get your mug down from the shelf for you. These two examples give members a sense of belonging.

5. **ADVOCATE.** Once you have members, you move them up the ladder to the next level – to that of advocate. An advocate is someone who sells you to other people. The criteria for an advocate are they will give referrals or promote you, and they keep buying. Advocates are one of your major capital assets.

6. **RAVING FAN.** Once you have created an advocate, you need to move them up to the top of the ladder where they become raving fans. Understand the difference: an advocate is someone who will sell for you whereas a raving fan is someone who can't stop selling for you. The exciting thing about raving fans is they can almost be regarded as part of your team. They want to see you succeed. Of course, they continue buying from you all along.

Remember, the aim of the game is to move people up from customer to raving fan. This is where you begin to make profit.

## Accounting

One of the first things you need to consider when setting up a new business is to set up the company's books. You could, of course, hire an accountant or bookkeeper and leave this all to them, but most people starting out initially will most probably want to do this themselves.

The easiest way to go about this, especially if you don't have an accounting background, is to purchase a computer-based bookkeeping software package. There are many good ones available that are also affordable. They will also teach you how to keep a set of books easily and accurately, and what's more, they have been designed so they provide all the information required at tax time.

You will need to make contact with a bookkeeper. It may be that, if you do the day-to-day bookkeeping functions yourself, you may only need the bookkeeper's services once a year at tax time. On the other hand, you may choose to use a bookkeeper on a monthly basis, or even full-time. Either way, find a good bookkeeper because you will need one.

Cashflow is one of the most important principles in business. I can't stress this enough. If you aren't focused on creating cashflow, then you're wasting your time in business. Anyone can create a business that's no more than just a job and that earns him or her a living, but very few will ever create a cashflow goldmine. If that's all that you're after, then you need to understand profit is the difference between cashflow in and cashflow out. And it's the in flow where you get exponential growth. To learn how to create instant cashflow, read my book Instant Cashflow – the Keys to Multiplying Your Business Profits.

## Operations

At this point, let's step back a little and consider the progress we have made in our quest to build up a company. Remember our basic goal is to BUY, BUILD and SELL. During the building phase, we set a vision of what we would like the business to look like at the end of our building phase. We also need to consider where we are at present.

OK, so we know where we want to get to all we need to do now is develop a plan on how to get there. We need an ACTION PLAN. We need to plan how we are going to grow and build the business so we can achieve our Vision.

Once we've created the plan, we need to list all the systems we'll need to put in place. Systems are part of the action plan. We need to implement systems to tell us how we do the various things we need to do to reach our vision. You see, once you systematize the business, it'll work without you. Remember, systems run the business, and people run the systems.

To systematize your business, start by analysing the major areas of your business. Take a good hard look at the following areas:

- **People and Education.**

Your business will only grow if your people do. So design an ongoing training system to ensure they acquire new knowledge all the time. Design and implement team member Positional Contracts and hold team skill-based sessions. Put in place a system that caters for redundancies. Develop a Social Club. Subscribe to educational newsletters and industry magazines and make them available to all your people. This will keep them abreast of developments and make them feel well informed.

Take care of new people from the moment they join your business by having in place an induction training program. And be sure to run regular team building training programs. Build career planning within the company, and set company and individual team member goals. Run Time Management Training and complete Positional 'How To' manuals.

Whenever you are dealing with people, the potential for conflict exists, so develop a system to resolve conflict. Develop, and publicize, your company's Rules of the Game – this will help minimize the potential for conflict within the work place.

Complete a consistent recruitment system and develop contingency staffing plans. Hold regular team meetings and develop a system for recognition and remuneration.

Use Behavioural, Personality and Communication Analysis with all team members – your *ACTION* BUSINESS COACH can assist you with this.

Set the company's Vision, write your Mission Statement, and make sure all your people get a copy. Your team can make or break your business. Develop the right environment and nurture your people through the development of effective, farsighted staffing plans and systems.

- **Delivery and Distribution.**

Wherever possible, run paperless systems in your business. Make sure you deliver your service with systematic consistency. If there's a way to make great service happen time after time, then make sure people are using it.

Have a look at your product packaging and make changes where necessary to ensure safer delivery. Forecast your stock movements so you'll always know what to order, when to order it and what money you'll have to spend. Identify those stock items that have the highest turnover and reorganise your stock so these items are easiest to get to and handle. Simplify your order pick and pack process. You see, if it's less time consuming to put away and then distribute stock, you'll save a bundle.

Complete a purchasing and stock receiving system, and consider outsourcing logistics and warehouse support. Specialist companies are often much better than you are at warehousing and distribution. Complete regular stocktakes and quantify your service or product delivery costs.

Measure the quality and professionalism of your service delivery because the more you measure it, the better it gets. It's a simple, yet effective, step. Follow up and measure the quality and time of deliveries. Your customers love on time, quality delivery, so make sure they're getting it.

Develop and institute a management system for freight, couriers and vehicles. Measure and use re-order levels; never order before you have to and never run out of stock. Use an order tracking system. Make sure every order is traceable, then if anything disappears you can start tracking it down.

Roster staff for service delivery, and increase your security. And always confirm the order and delivery details are correct before you deliver a product or service. Make sure you use a 'Just In Time' stock delivery system so you not only get the stock but you also get it just before it's needed.

- **Testing and Measuring.**

Complete and keep to monthly and yearly budgets so you'll know where your business is going as regularly as possible. Measure the conversion rates for each sales person. That way you'll know where you've got to improve and exactly how you're performing.

Complete a purchasing system for all internal purchases. And always complete a Marketing Campaign Profit Analysis so you'll know where you're making money and where you're loosing it.

Have a system in place to deal with petty cash. Keep a record of profit margins. Know what your big margin products and services are and focus on them. It's not just about turnover, it's also about profit.

Continuously measure the number of leads you get and where they come from. Few businesses know how many leads they get each week. Even fewer know where those leads came from. Develop a database and keep in regular contact with them. You also need to continuously monitor your credit control and the age of your accounts.

Measure your average dollar sale for every team member and record the number of transactions for each customer. Complete a monthly balance sheet and measure the Key Performance Indicators in all areas of the company. Also make sure weekly bank reconciliations are completed and daily or weekly update cashflow statements are done.

Have a daily banking system and complete regular stock control check-ups because you've got to make sure the numbers are always accurate. Complete all regular government returns. Nothing will hit harder than a government return not lodged on time. Keep an asset register that includes depreciation. Know what you own, serial numbers and all. Most importantly, you need to know how much it's worth.

Work with an external accountant for tax planning, and have a system for payroll and superannuation.

- **Systems and Technology.**

Schedule and complete regular maintenance on all equipment operated by your company. Rather than waiting until your machinery crashes, get it serviced in times of low need.

Use computer invoicing and credit monitoring. It'll save you time and money, and you'll be sure everything is consistent.

Document and picture all tasks in an operations manual. This should cover what needs to be done, when it needs to be done, who should do it, what the standards are and how to measure the results. Run a computerized stock control system and complete systems training and induction programs – you see training how to use a good system takes about a tenth the time it takes to teach people how to do the job.

Use the latest computer programs whenever possible and complete a phone/fax systems upgrade. Go through and regularly update quality control and quality assurance. Be sure to run a computer back-up system as this can save you a mountain of time should the worst happen to your computers. And run both internal and external E-Mail systems.

Document and chart all workflow processes, document all sales and marketing systems and information flow processes using a purpose-designed computer database program.

Network all of your company's computers for ease of access. Also use rosters and schedules for repetitive tasks around the office - that way routine tasks will get done without anyone really noticing so the focus can remain on the customer.

Complete a Policies and Procedure Manual. If everything's written down, duplication is a simple step and you're reliant on the system, not the people. Prioritize extraordinary tasks as they can be time-consuming and costly to deal with. Can your system cope? And remember, as you company grows, your systems may be tested to the limit of their original design capabilities, rendering them outdated, inefficient or unable to cope. Redesign your systems as your company grows.

Once you have the systems in place, only then do you source the people to work in the business. Avoid getting your people first otherwise you'll end up with chaos. And remember the Kaizen principal. Seek to constantly improve your operation.

# Part 6

# ▌Selling the Business

At the beginning of this book I mentioned to be RICH you need to have two things that will allow you to produce the third. I mentioned you need a rather large CASHFLOW as well as a solid physical ASSET base. These two things combined allow you to create the third part of getting RICH ... PAPER ASSETS ...

Now, I know most people would be happy with being just WEALTHY ... you know, lots of PASSIVE income and lots of physical ASSETS. That's fine. And it's easily achievable by buying, building and selling businesses.

But remember, the only reason you start a business is to sell it.

Generally speaking, you won't become RICH by owning just one company – you need to buy, build and sell businesses a few times over A good strategy is to hang on to your first business for its passive income stream while you acquire and build up your next business. You will be able to do this because your first business will by now be running without you. You will have the time to devote to finding and building your next business. Expect to consider between 50 to 100 businesses before you settle on just one. When it comes time to sell your business, you'll need to be a good negotiator. You're going to be aiming to get a far higher price for your business than anyone else might if they were selling it simply because you've finished building it. The buyer just has to move in and start trading. Everything has been set up already.

You'll advertise your business for sale, using the best medium according to your individual situation. If you need help, call an **ACTION** Business Coach – they are specialists and can help you design an ad that works. Then you'll wait for prospective buyers to make contact.

They'll want to see your operation, and they'll want to go through your books and talk about future potential. They'll then make an offer and expect to negotiate. But more about this later ...

At this point, I'd like to remind you about the only reason you got started in the first place. You want to ultimately build up a passive income stream that will give you the ability to become self-sufficient - to become wealthy – to become rich. You have to think of yourself as a Business Trader, not just a Business Builder. Got it? You are aiming to Buy, Build and Sell, NOT Buy, Build and Hold.

There may well be other times when you decide to hold on to a business for a while, and that's fine. You could be planning to franchise the business, for example. Again, more on that a little later on.

## Finishing It First

What do I mean when I say FINISHING the business? You've finished building the business when you have achieved your vision for it. When it operates or functions as you originally dreamed it would when you first bought it or established it from scratch. Basically it is finished when all the systems are in place, allowing it to run without you. And there are very good reasons for finishing a business. Firstly, you will get a high price for it when you sell. Secondly, because it's now a finished business you can sell it through a broker, who will attract buyers with larger budgets. And thirdly, because the business is producing a passive income stream, you won't be under any pressure to sell. You have the luxury of holding it until you get your price.

Some of the things I set up as goals when I start building the business are the following:

1. I want to know what my turnover will be on the day I finish building it.

2. I want to know what my profit is on the day I finish building it.

3. I want to know what the date will be when I will finish building the business.

4. I want to know what the sale price will be on the day I finish building it.

Your business will now be worth considerably more than when you first bought it. You will be aiming to get what it's worth – a very different scenario to when you were considering buying it in the first place.

Because the profit was built into the buying price, not the selling price, you'll be holding out for your price. That's the beauty of it. You will be able to afford to sit tight until the right deal comes along. The business will be running along very nicely without you being there. You can be spending your time sifting through likely businesses to buy next. Remember the definition of a business? It's a commercial, profitable enterprise that works without you.

So when is it you can you walk away from your business? You can walk away from it as soon as you have all the systems in place, and as soon as you have a fully trained team. The business will now be running itself. If it doesn't, or if snags occur, then you will need to fine-tune some of the systems. This in itself will be a good thing because it will be testing your systems and people in real-time situations. Once you iron out all the teething problems, you should have a foolproof business.

Businesses that run themselves will be attractive to investors for the very reason they don't want to become tied down to running the show in the first place. That's why they call themselves investors and not sole operators or things like that. The fact you have developed and implemented all these systems will be very appealing to the investor.

However, it is possible for a buyer to come along and who intends running the business himself or herself. I call this selling to a Technician.

These buyers are looking to buy themselves a job, and that's fine, if that's what they want.

With these buyers, if they are the only ones you get, be prepared to think about offering Vendor Finance. It may just make the difference between making a sale at a very good price, or hoping for a sale and not being sure.

## Set a High Price

The aim of the game is to get a very good price for your finished business. After all, not only is this now the way you will be making money, but the buyer will be benefiting from all your knowledge, hard work, foresight and risk-taking.

My advice here is this: PICK A PRICE AND DOUBLE IT …

Yes, I know this sounds a bit rich. Pick yourself up off the floor and let me explain.

You are selling your dream, right? What's more, you are not just selling a business, you are selling one that WORKS. You are selling a business that has been set up so well it can be duplicated anywhere in the world. You see, this is because everything works – the marketing works, the systems work, the people work - everything works to create the results. This is all guaranteed because you have built a definable relationship here. Your database will show exactly what is happening in the business. It will show whom your customers are, how many times they buy from you, and what the average dollar spend is. Think of it this way; you are selling the rights to duplicate this business worldwide as well as any future income the business might deliver.

Also, negotiations always begin from the price. Buyers have to start somewhere.  They will evaluate your business against the asking price and negotiate from there. Ask too low, and they will still negotiate down from that low price. Remember this; buyers decide based on price, not value.

## Vendor Finance

Vendor finance is a very useful option you need to bear in mind when selling your finished business. This is particularly so the higher the price you are asking. In many instances, a buyer may not have ready access to a very large amount of money, but he or she might still be the perfect buyer for your business. And it might also be that, for whatever reason, the banks may not be a viable option for them.

Vendor financing often allows for a fast sale, as there are no lengthy delays while the traditional lenders study the finance application in detail.

Very often this is the only way to get your price. Buyers may well consider vendor finance as attractive because there may be no interest charges built in. You might offer a straight deal involving a set number of monthly repayments until the purchase price has been met.

Vendor finance also means there may be no capital gains to be taken into account. And the terms of the deal might ensure you keep an income stream from the business flowing that much longer. If the worst came to the worse, you could even state in the contract that, should things not run according to plan, you would get your business back. You would then have earned the monthly repayments along the way as well.

## Management Buyout

Management buyouts are becoming an increasingly popular way of selling finished businesses. People running and working in a business often see ways of doing things better and of making improvements, if only the company were theirs.

Many too dream of owning their own business some day, and buying out the business that currently employs them means they don't have to leave and get involved with the unknown. They have always wanted to be the boss, and this could be the chance they have been waiting for. There is security in familiarity. Others could fear loosing their job if someone else buys the business and appoints their own management team to run it. A management buyout could be a way of ensuring job security.

The question you have to ask yourself as a seller in this situation is can they raise the money?

If the business has been built and run properly, it will be producing good profits. Banks might be willing to finance a management buyout, particularly if the bank in question is the business' bank and therefore has a long relationship with it.

Vendor Finance is also always an option to consider.

## Find an Employee with a Payout

The best buyer in the world is an employee with a payout. This could be an insurance payout, or a retrenchment payout from a previous employer. By buying the business, it could allow them to just keep on doing things the way they always have. It offers safety and security. And by working in the business themselves they could save having to pay a wage.

## Sell One Part at a Time

Sometimes breaking up a business into smaller parts will make it easier to sell. Selling it off one piece at a time, whether to the same buyer or different ones, can very often be an excellent sales strategy.

You might consider selling the business according to different territories or geographic areas. You might consider splitting it up into segments. For instance, if the business is a discount retail store, you might sell off the computer section separately to the white good section. You might sell the furniture section separately to the audio and television section. You could also sell off parts of the business as you finish building them.

## Flog it

Sometimes you buy a business just to realize a quick profit selling it again a short time later. These quick cash sales are a useful way of raising capital fast for use in other business ventures. It could be you've come across an opportunity that is too good to pass on.

The key to these opportunistic deals is to buy low and resell quickly. You don't want to hang on to these businesses too long. You also wouldn't spend any time or money finishing these businesses – you'd only fix them so they are more sellable.

The general idea here is to keep your operating costs to a minimum so you can maximize your profit. Don't get an Ad Agency to design your Business For Sale advertisement – do it yourself. Read my best selling book Cash, Customers, and Ads That Sell to find out how to write the most effective ad.

And finally, it's important you sell yourself. You see, prospective buyers won't be too happy about buying a business you've had for only a short time unless they are happy it has passed through YOUR hands first. They must become convinced it will be passing from you in a far better position than that in which you acquired it.

## Franchise or License it

The ULTIMATE SALE has to be to franchise the business or to license it. You see, when you have developed a sound business that works, it can be duplicated at little or no extra cost. You can sell the business time and time again to different people all over the world. And the beauty of this is there's no limit to the number of times you can sell it.

Think of some of the most popular businesses today, and chances are they're either franchises or they're business that operate under license. Take McDonalds, for instance. McDonalds is a fast food franchise that operates all over the world today. The potential is enormous, as there could just about be one in every suburb in the world. Each franchisee has his or her own unique territory in which to operate. This ensures the franchisees do not compete with each other.

The franchise market is a dynamic industry that allows any type of business to grow by distributing its products or services. When your business expands by selling its trademark and business systems to other people, you are adopting the franchise structure. And by granting permission as a manufacturer to a distributor or retailer to sell your products, you create the contract of a franchise.

If you run a profitable business and are contemplating franchising, the first thing you need to decide is whether your product range or service is flexible enough to adapt to future trends. The next thing you need to decide is whether you want to franchise your business yourself, or whether you want to call in an expert business to do it for you. I'd recommend the latter for a host of reasons, not least of which is it's a complex field full of pitfalls and legalities that may not be immediately apparent. You can check out my web site www.franchisemasters.com.au for more information.

Franchise Masters develop franchise systems that will encourage long-term growth and profitability. They will also advise you which franchising model best suit your situation.

But before you decide on whether to franchise or not, you need to consider whether this route suits you. Ask yourself the following questions:

- Do you see yourself as always striving for excellence?

- Do you possess a leadership style that can supervise and motivate a large number of people?

- Would you enjoy acting as a mentor to a large number of people?

- Are you happy to participate in forums and group activities, which could involve travel away from home?

- Are you happy to invest the money and time to continually learn new knowledge and skills to ensure franchise system's growth?

- Are you happy to forgo your own way of doing things and follow someone else's systems?

- Are you hungry to grow your business?

- Do you have what it takes?

If you decide franchising is for you, you will need to ensure your franchise and all documentation and recommendations complies with the Franchising Code of Conduct. Effective disclosure documentation is often the catalyst for a successful franchise. You will need to ensure you have detailed disclosure documentation to ensure your franchise model is compliant with the Franchise Consumer Code and provides the potential franchisee a "no secrets" approach to buying the business. So what's the difference then between operating as a franchisee and operating as a licensee?

Basically, when you buy a franchise, you buy not only a branded business, but also the entire system with which you can run the business in the intended manner. You get all the training necessary not only to get you up and running, but also to keep you up-to-date on an on-going basis. You get all the documentation, all the reporting mechanisms and all the backing necessary to keep your performance levels in line with that which the franchise owner demands.

Operating as a licensee, you only get the rights to manufacture and/or market a particular product or line of products. How you set up and run your business remains your business. Major pharmaceutical products and cosmetics manufacturers often opt for this method.

Both options include regular paperwork that needs to be filled in and lodged. And of course, if you are operating as a franchisee or licensee, you will need to pay royalties to the owner on a regular basis.

This is what is so attractive about selling your business this way. You get to receive royalties on a regular basis. This is your CASH COW.

So, what's keeping you? Get your business started and sell …

## Go Public

Going Public is THE BIG GAME. It's the serious stuff that all true entrepreneurs aim for. It's the game that can make you seriously rich. It's also the game for Entrepreneurs Only.

You Go Public for two reasons. Firstly you might want to raise capital to fund a future expansion project or to fund the development of a new line of products. Going Public is an excellent way to raise a very large amount of money as quickly as possible. Secondly, you can Go Public as a way of selling out. It is the ultimate way of getting the maximum price possible for your business, especially when you're unsure as to what that maximum price might be. Much like auctioning your house.

Going Public is nevertheless a very expensive option to take. There are certain administrative requirements that have to be adhered to. Compliance costs money.

Of course, there is a cheaper option, if that's a major concern. You could always consider becoming an unlisted company. This way, you don't get to list on the Stock Exchange like all the other listed companies do; you simply sell shares in your company to a limited number of private shareholders. That way you still realize a price for your company, but you get to keep control. Listed companies, on the other hand, are owned by the shareholders, and managed by a management team. The public can buy shares in the business through the stock exchange. Stockbrokers do the buying and selling on your behalf.

Playing the Share Price Game now becomes what it is all about. Shareholders want a return on their investment, and it's up to the business' management team to ensure they get the sort of return they want.

## My Last Four Entrepreneurial Secrets

When you think about it, my last four secrets are all common sense really. It's all very simple and straightforward. And the beauty is you can apply them to your everyday life as well, not just to your business.

So, what are these secrets?

### Leverage

If you think you can earn more by working a little harder, it's time for a reality check. Take a look around you. Thousands of people you know all work hard, but are they all really getting anywhere? No, of course they're not.

The aim of the game isn't to work harder; it's to create better results with less effort. It's about finding ways of achieving more with less.

The key to success is LAZINESS…

This may sound controversial, so let me explain. You need to continually leverage your time, your efforts, your money and your knowledge.

If you're paid an hourly wage, you'll never earn more than the number of hours you work, but if your business is set up so you're paid whether you work or not, you'll truly understand one of the key principles of success – Leverage.

Leverage is simply the ability to do more with less.

Put it this way; employees earn money, business owners make money and investors and entrepreneurs collect money.

It's all about creating an income stream that flows whether you work or not. And creating one that gets better all the time.

## Sell Pans

I can't tell you how many times people who have invented something approach me. They say: "I've invented this fantastic gadget that the market will just love it. It will make millions. Are you interested?" My answer is always the same – NO.

Now don't get me wrong – I have nothing against inventors. But let me give you an example to illustrate my position. Back in the gold rush days when everyone was out there digging away in attempt to find riches, would I, had I been there, have bought a prospector's license? No, most definitely not.

What would I have done, you ask? I would have set up a stall on the side of the road and sold pans. You see, every single one of the diggers would have needed a pan.

Let me put it another way. Do you think you can make a better burger than McDonald's can? Of course. But can you come up with a better system for selling burgers?

Interesting, isn't it?

My advice is this: don't go against the trend. Don't try to sell to people who don't want to buy. Rather stand by the road and sell to people who desperately want to buy. You only need one thing to make a fortune in the restaurant business – a starving crowd.

If you've got a product or service everyone wants, then it'll sell itself. Marketing is so simple when you stand in the path of people who really want to buy rather than you having to go out there to sell.

## Knowledge

In today's world, you can't be cheaper than your competitors for long. You can't be far better than anyone for long, so you've got to know knowledge is the key to business success.

You must ensure you READ, READ, READ. You can't read too much. I have read over 700 books on business. How many have you?

Get yourself a great mentor – someone who has succeeded in business. Learn from a winner, not a D-grade player. Consider this: coaches and advisors surround every great sports star, business person and superstar. And, as the world of business moves faster and gets more competitive, you can't possibly hope to keep up with both the changes in your industry as well as the innovations in sales, marketing and management strategies. Many now consider having a business coach a necessity, not a luxury.

On top of all that, it's impossible to get an objective answer from yourself. Now don't get me wrong, you can survive in business without the help of a coach, but it's almost impossible to thrive.

A coach can see the forest for the trees. A coach will make you focus on the game. A coach will make you run more laps than you feel like running. A coach will tell it like it is. A coach will give you small pointers. A coach will listen. A coach will also be your sales manager, your marketing director, your training co-ordinator, your partner, your mentor, and your best friend. Furthermore, an *ACTION* Business Coach will help you make your dreams come true.

You need to attend business seminars. Not only will you learn amazing things that apply directly to your business and your life, but you'll also receive much needed motivation to help you through the hard times. Your batteries will be recharged. And you'll find it a great place to network.

One other thing – don't be afraid to make mistakes. Develop a culture that allows you to make mistakes, because if you don't, you'll never know just where your boundaries lie. You'll also never discover new or better ways of doing things. The only reason I know more than most people is I've made more mistakes than them. Remember the first time you learnt to walk? How many times did you fall down? Did you just give up because it was all too hard? No, you kept on trying until you got it right. Then you learnt how to run.

It still amazes me to this day how a business is a reflection of its owner. Some owners want to control everything, and wonder why none of their team takes any initiative. Some hate selling and love paperwork, so they always get their numbers done but never seem to sell much. Remember – you only ever get the staff you deserve. The same is true of your private life. It wasn't until I became a great person, a great businessman and a great leader that I started to attract great people.

Anyone with teenage kids will know one thing about them – they KNOW everything. Just ask them if you don't believe me. But it's what you learn when you think you know everything that really counts.

Intelligence is the ability to draw even finer and finer distinctions on a certain subject. Remember how that book you read twice was different the second time round? One of the fastest ways to make sure you never learn anything new, never grow and never create more income for yourself is to continually state you know everything. Open your mind. It's not the major revelations that will make you a fortune; it's the finer distinctions that will give you the edge over the rest of the population.

The difference between ordinary and extraordinary is that little bit of extra.

## Profit is KING

The Number One business rule is PROFIT IS KING. The success of your business has nothing whatsoever to do with how much revenue it makes or how many people you employ. And it also has nothing to do with what market share it enjoys. It's all about profit.

Now I would suggest you take a moment to consider what business you are in. Most business people define their business by what they sell. A motorcar dealership, for instance, would say they are in the motor business. However, if they were to take a marketing view, they would soon realize they are actually in the profit-making business.

Making a profit is as simple as spending less than you earn. In other words, you've got to buy customers with your sales and marketing efforts for less than they spend with you. It's fairly basic maths, but it isn't being taught in too many business schools.

# In Conclusion

I have now given you the keys to success. These keys will unlock success in any business, and they are just waiting for you to make use of them.

The keys to your success as a business person and as an entrepreneur, are there to enable you to jump in whole-heartedly.

The choice is yours – take it or leave it. It's as simple as that.

The first stage in your quest for riches is to develop a passive income stream. The next stage is to become wealthy. Wealth comes when you not only have PASSIVE income, but you also have assets to back it up. Wealth comes when you've truly cemented your long-term passive income with the steadiness of physical asset growth.

Beyond wealth lies rich. Rich usually comes through only one thing; paper assets. To be rich you need to have a rather large cashflow and a solid physical asset base.

You'll need to consider your cashflow as you travel down this road to riches. Where will it come from? There is only one tool I recommend you use for creating cashflow in your life… your own business. To get rich, and to get rich fast, you need more cashflow.  More, so you can buy more assets at a much faster pace. I recommend you get into business for cashflow and then to use the money you make to invest in property.

Remember my definition of a business? It's A Commercial, Profitable, Enterprise that Works Without Me. But there are many different levels to 'being in business'. These I call The 5 Levels of Entrepreneurs. These Levels are a framework of the steps you need to take and the thought processes and tools you'll need as you progress from Level Zero (an employee) to becoming self-employed as a Level 1, then up to Level 2 as a Manager, Level 3 as the Owner/Leader of the business, and finally, breaking through the all-important barrier to Level 4 (Investor) and Level 5 (Entrepreneur).

As a Level 4 Investor, your motto will be Buy Build and Sell, and that's exactly what you'll be doing as you create amazing wealth.

I have shown you the three ways of buying a business (starting it yourself, buying retail or buying wholesale) and when each is most appropriate as you progress along the road to riches. You now also know where to find the best businesses and how to raise the money you'll need to buy them. I've also given you the secrets to doing amazing No Money Down Deals.

But perhaps more importantly, you also know my seven rules for buying a business. You see, rules are by far and away the most important part of any investor's success. With a good set of rules you'll be able to consistently create a winning investment result.

Once you've selected a business to buy, you'll need to brush up your negotiating skills as everything will now depend on how well you do the deal. You'll know to leave your emotions at home, and you'll know how to walk away from a deal. But you'll also know how to do the best deals possible.

Once you've bought the business, you've got to build it up so it can produce for you a passive income stream. Of course, there are only five things to do to grow a business, you'll know exactly where to start and what to do. Once you have begun that process, it'll be time for you to concentrate on other areas of business as well. Areas such as marketing, team building, customer service, accounting and operations.

When you decide it's time to sell your business, you'll know exactly how to go about it. You'll know what it takes to finish a business, how to ensure you can set a high price for it, and what options are available to you as a vendor. You'll understand, for instance, the advantages of vendor finance, management buyouts, and selling the business one part at a time. You'll also know all about what it takes to franchise or license a business and what's involved in going public.

I've given you my four entrepreneurial secrets – these are secrets you can use in your everyday life as well because they are simple and universal.

I've given you the knowledge that will allow you to create the results you want. It's your choice whether to run with it or not.

Make the choice. Take the step.

I say to everyone: You've only got one life. You only have one chance to create an amazing result for yourself. There's only one chance. Don't throw it away. Live the life you want to live, the way you want to live it.

Be all you want to be.

The keys are here ... will you choose to use them?

# ■ RECOMMENDED READING LIST

"The only difference between YOU now and YOU in 5 years time will be the people you meet and the books you read..." Charlie 'tremendous' Jones.

"And, the only difference between YOUR income now and YOUR income in 5 years time will be the people you meet, the books you read, the tapes you listen to, and then how YOU apply it all..." Brad Sugars

- My Life in Advertising & Scientific Advertising by Claude Hopkins
- Tested Advertising Methods, or any other books by John Caples
- Write Language by Paul Dunn & Alan Pease
- 22 Immutable Laws of Marketing, or any other books by Al Reis & Jack Trout
- Ogilvy on Advertising, or any other books by David Ogilvy
- 21 Ways to Build a Referral Based Business by Brad Sugars
- 21 Ways to Increase Your Advertising Response by Mark Tier
- Any books by Murray Raphel
- Any books by Jay Abraham
- The Great Sales Book  by Jack Collis
- Brad Sugars Competitive Edge Video Series Includes Workbook
- Brad Sugars "Introduction to Sales & Marketing" 3 hour Video
- Brad Sugars Competitive Edge 2-day Workshop Audio Cassettes
- Leverage – Business Board Game by Brad Sugars
- Brad Sugars "Instant Cashflow" Book
- Brad Sugars "Cash, Customers and Ads that Sell ..." Book
- 17 Ways to Increase Your Business Profits booklet & tape by Brad Sugars. FREE OF CHARGE to Business Owners ... call now for your copy ...

**\*To order products from the recommended reading list call *ACTION International* on +61 (0) 7 3368 2525**

# ■ ATTENTION BUSINESS OWNERS ...

Here's how you can have one of Brad's *ACTION* Business Coaches guide you to success ...

With your own business in mind, go through the following list of business opportunities/challenges and mark the top five that apply to you. If you'd like you can even add another in the space provided. One of the team will be in touch and work through these challenges with you. We'll offer you a list of possible solutions, of course recommending the fastest ways to get to your goals, then it's time to get to work on creating your own entrepreneurial success ... So, read this list and let us know the biggest areas of opportunity in your business ...

## Don't Delay... We can help you become more profitable NOW!

- Having a strategy that will compel my former and inactive customers and clients to again buy from me with enthusiasm and fervor.

- A step by step marketing plan that will significantly increase my customers and clients without taking my time and energy from day to day business.

- Having effective and inexpensive ways to generate more leads and more prospects to my business.

- Strong Yellow Pages advertising that compels prospects to my business

- The most effective sales appeal for my product or service that in the eyes of potential customers will uniquely put my business head and shoulders above my competition.

- To effectively use the telephone to produce more customers and more clients for my business or practice.

- To quickly and efficiently sell to companies that may have hard to reach decision-makers.

- To become a more effective consultant or professional advisor in my field.

- To write customer focussed advertising copy that will draw willing customers, new and old to my business.

- A unique and effective system that will turn my best customers into my best sales people, referring me new people all the time, while still being my best customers.

- To create and execute an irresistible direct mail campaign that will turn my mailbox into a profit centre.

- Having a systematic can't miss way to get my customers to buy again and again.

- To gain more impetus and motivation for me and my team, to really put into place strategies that will get things going.

Comments:_____

**Fax completed form to *ACTION* on +61 (0) 7 3368 2535 or forward to your nearest *ACTION* Office (see following pg).**

# ■ ACTION CONTACT DETAILS:

**ACTION** International **Australia**
GPO Box 1340, Brisbane QLD 4001
Ph: 61 (0) 7 3368 2525
Free Call: 1800 670 335
Fax: 61 (0) 7 3368 2535

**ACTION** International **Asia**
171 Tras Street
#08-177 Union Building
Singapore 079025
Ph: 65 6 221 0100
Fax: 65 6 221 0200

**ACTION** International **USA**
**ACTION** International, Inc.
5670 Wynn Road Suite C
Las Vegas, Nevada 89118
Ph: 1 (702) 795 3188
Free Call: (888) 483 2828
Fax: 1 (702) 795 3183

**ACTION** International **New Zealand**
PO Box 25 651, St. Heliers, New Zealand
Ph: 64 (0) 9 575 5790
Free Call: 0800 369 888
Fax: 64 (0) 9 575 5791

**ACTION** International **Canada**
231, 6707 Elbow Drive SW
Calgary Alberta T2V-0E5
Ph: 1 (403) 259 5546
Free Call: (877) 303 5546
Fax: 1 (403) 259 5921

**ACTION** International **Mexico**
Saucos 708, Colonial de la Sierra
Garza Garcia, Nuevo Leon, Mexico 66286
Ph: 52 (818) 303 3861
Fax: 52 (818) 303 3862

**ACTION** International
**United Kingdom**
Office 407, MWB Business Exchange,
26-28 Hammersmith Grove,
London W6 7BA
Ph: 44 (0) 208 600 1874
Fax: 44 (0) 208 834 1100

**ACTION** International **Malaysia**
10 Jalan SS 1/25,
47301 Petaling Jaya, Selangor Darul Ihsan
West Malaysia
Ph: 60 (0) 3 7877 8614
Fax: 60 (0) 3 7877 8671

**ACTION** International **Indonesia**
Jl. Jend. Sudirman Kav. 1
Wisma 46, Kota BNI, 43rd Floor,
Jakarta 10220, Indonesia
Ph: 62 (0) 21 574 8880
Fax: 62 (0) 21 574 8886

# ▌ LEVERAGE - THE GAME OF BUSINESS...

## The rewards start flowing the moment you start playing ...

That's what LEVERAGE is all about.

Three hours of fun, learning and becoming an amazingly successful business person. It's a breakthrough in education, that'll have you racking up the profits in no time. The principles you take away from playing this game, You'll want to play it again & again will set you up for a life of business success. It'll alter your perception and open your mind to what's truly possible. Sit back and watch your profits soar ...

It's time you had the edge over your competition ...

Leverage has been played by all age groups from 12-85 and has been a huge learning experience for all ... the most common comment being "I thought I knew a lot, and just by playing a simple board game I have realized I have a long way to go," The knowledge I've gained from playing Leverage will make me thousands. Thanks for the lesson ...'

Leverage retails at AUD$295.00 ...

**To order your copy contact your local *ACTION* Business Coach or call *ACTION International* on :**

*ACTION International* Australia & New Zealand +61 (0) 7 3368 2525

Freecall within Australia 1800 670 335

Freecall within New Zealand 0800 440 335

Asia +(65) 6221 0100

United States of America +1 702 795 3188 or Freecall (888) 483 2828

Canada +1 403 259 5546

Europe +44 (0) 20 8600 1874

# ▮ INSTANT CASHFLOW...

## The Keys to Multiplying your Business Profits...

Learn Brad's most amazingly powerful and user-friendly sales and marketing tips all in one book. Previously this material was only available at one of Brad's high-level workshops. You will read this book once then refer to it again and again! There are so many simple, easy and ready to use tips on how to boost your bottom line that you'll have to refer it to your family and friends as well.

Instant Cashflow retails at AUD$29.95 ...

**To order your copy contact your local *ACTION* Business Coach or call *ACTION International* on :**

*ACTION International* Australia & New Zealand +61 (0) 7 3368 2525

Freecall within Australia 1800 670 335

Freecall within New Zealand 0800 440 335

Asia +(65) 6221 0100

United States of America +1 702 795 3188 or Freecall (888) 483 2828

Canada +1 403 259 5546

Europe +44 (0) 20 8600 1874

# ▌Cash, Customers & Ads That Sell ...

### 149 Hints, Tips and Strategies on Writing Ads that Sell ...

You'll never write another BAD advertisement again! Armed with all of Brads' super  powerful advertising hints, tips and insider trade secrets you'll be ready to write super profitable ads in no time at all ...

Co-written with "AD Man" Trevor Mayhew this book is a must for anyone serious about their entrepreneurial business success.

You'll quickly learn how to create profitable strategies and then the ads that make the strategies work...You'd be mad to pass up the opportunity to get this book!

Cash, Customers & Ads That Sell ... retails at AUD$29.95 ...

### To order your copy contact your local *ACTION* Business Coach or call *ACTION International* on :

*ACTION International* Australia & New Zealand +61 (0) 7 3368 2525

Freecall within Australia 1800 670 335

Freecall within New Zealand 0800 440 335

Asia +(65) 6221 0100

United States of America +1 702 795 3188 or Freecall (888) 483 2828

Canada +1 403 259 5546

Europe +44 (0) 20 8600 1874

# ▌Entrepreneurs Training ... Where You Discover How to Make Your Wildest Dreams a Reality ...

**And, here's why we won't let most people attend this training program ...**

Never before has there been a workshop like this. Presented by entrepreneur and marketing guru Brad Sugars, this workshop will teach you everything you'll ever need to know about personal wealth, lifestyle and business success. It will change your life in the most positive way imaginable.

The Entrepreneurs Training is not open to everyone. In fact, it's open only to those who share a common goal - the desire to succeed.

Whether you're looking to make the most of your personal wealth, or increase the cashflow of your business, this 5 day, live-in workshop, will provide you with memorable gifts that will remain with you for the rest of your life.

This workshop is strictly invitation only. You'll need more than just money and time to attend this course. You'll need to embrace the workshop's motto - 'Whatever it takes'.   100% full on from the word go, you'll work hard, play hard and learn the level of performance you'll need to work at to create the entrepreneurial success you're after ...

If you could imagine what it would be like to achieve everything you've ever dreamt of, and have 100% trust in yourself, you'll understand why the Action Entrepreneurs Training is strictly Employees Not Allowed. You can never live in a state of fear, or work from an unleveraged place again after you've lived through these 5 days ...

You don't make a fortune running businesses, you make a fortune selling them. Discover how to take every business you have and turn it into capital growth. Unlike property, shares or any other form of investment, you can massively increase the value of your investment in a very short space of time, reaping the rewards both along the way and when you sell.

This workshop will do more than simply teach you how to make money. It's about discovering who you are, and who you want to be. You're guaranteed to get more out of The Entrepreneurs Workshop than any other workshop you've been to in the past.

**This workshop is an absolute must. Call** *ACTION International* **TODAY to reserve your place +61 (0)7 3368 2525.**

*ACTION International* Australia & New Zealand +61 (0) 7 3368 2525

Freecall within Australia 1800 670 335

Freecall within New Zealand 0800 440 335

Asia +(65) 6221 0100

United States of America +1 702 795 3188 or Freecall (888) 483 2828

Canada +1 403 259 5546
Europe +44 (0) 20 8600 1874

# ▌ Get Stacks of CASH and Heaps of CUSTOMERS ...

## ... get your ads designed by our Champion Creative Team ...

As you've just seen there's a lot to remember when it comes to writing effective ads. Well imagine having a team of marketing professionals design your ads for you ...

You will have some of the best in the country writing and designing your ads for you. Professionals who have created thousands of profitable advertisements and marketing campaigns.

Imagine having a Yellow Pages ad that has your phone ringing off the hook, or a Print Ad that has customers flocking through your door. Maybe you'd like an irresistible Sales Script that make prospects feel compelled to buy, or a Referral Strategy that generates hundreds of qualified, cost effective new leads. Our team of copywriters and graphic artists can give you all this and more ...

You can have our Champion Creative Team design a Web-site that will have the orders flooding in, or a Direct Mail campaign that turns your mail box into an amazing profit generating centre. If you're looking to change your image, imagine having our Champion Creative Team design your new Corporate Image or Logo. Best of all we give you a dozen variations on your ads for you to test and measure, so you can be sure to find one that gets amazing results.

Our team is not focussed on being 'clever' or winning awards. For years they've honed their skills in creating campaigns with one goal in mind ... Making Our Clients MONEY.

Being in business is not about doing it all yourself, it's about Leverage. It's about getting outside professionals doing the work for you, so your time is free to focus on growing your business and reaping the rewards. So why spend hours trying to design ads yourself, when you can have our creative team put together a sales and profit focused campaign that will have the money rolling in, in no time.

**Call our team TODAY on 1800 11 33 44 or +61 7 3367 322, or visit us on the web www.ai-design.com.au, and have us get started on your MONEY MAKING Campaign NOW.**

# ⬛ ATTENTION BUSINESS OWNERS ...
## increase your business profits

Here's how you can have one of Brad's *ACTION* Business Coaches guide you to success ...

Like every successful sporting icon or team, a business needs a coach to help it achieve it full potential. In order to guarantee your business success you can have one of Brad's teams as your business coach. You will learn about how you can get amazing business results with the help of the team at *ACTION International*.

The business coaches are ready to take you and your business on a journey that will reward you for the rest of your life. You see, we believe *ACTION* speaks louder than words.

Complete & post this card to discover how the team at *ACTION* can help you increase your income today ...

### *ACTION International...*Business Trainers and Consultants ...
### ... Because being in business should give YOU more life ...

Name . . . . . . . . . . . . . . . . . . . . . . . . . . . . . . . . . . . . . . . . . . . . . . . . . . . . . . . . . . . .

Position . . . . . . . . . . . . . . . . . . . . . . . . . . . . . . . . . . . . . . . . . . . . . . . . . . . . . . . . . .

Company . . . . . . . . . . . . . . . . . . . . . . . . . . . . . . . . . . . . . . . . . . . . . . . . . . . . . . . . .

Address . . . . . . . . . . . . . . . . . . . . . . . . . . . . . . . . . . . . . . . . . . . . . . . . . . . . . . . . . . .


Phone . . . . . . . . . . . . . . . . . . . . . . . . . . . . . . . . . . . . . . . . . . . . . . . . . . . . . . . . . . . .

Fax . . . . . . . . . . . . . . . . . . . . . . . . . . . . . . . . . . . . . . . . . . . . . . . . . . . . . . . . . . . . . .

Email . . . . . . . . . . . . . . . . . . . . . . . . . . . . . . . . . . . . . . . . . . . . . . . . . . . . . . . . . . . .

Referred by . . . . . . . . . . . . . . . . . . . . . . . . . . . . . . . . . . . . . . . . . . . . . . . . . . . . . . .